Being Vegetarian for Life

by
Jennifer Stang

Catalog-in-Publication Data on File

ISBN: 978-0-9894397-1-8

Published by
William Baughman Publishing
1443 S. Curson Ave.
Los Angeles, CA 90019
323.546.9490
williambaughman.com

Print v1i

Table of Contents

My Inspiration

In the several years that Santa Barbara, California has been my home, I have been inspired by the power of this land's natural beauty -- for who would not aspire to a healthier way of life when the air breathed is crispy-delicious, the fresh waters for bathing refresh the pores, and the majestic surrounding mountains provide serene respite for the soul?

And very specially...

it is with the utmost love that I dedicate this book to my mother, whose wisdom, strength, and unending love have nourished me, to my effervescent father, whose verve and confidence inspire me, to my brilliantly creative brother-companion of my heart, and to my patient, ever-supportive and loving husband, Jim.

Jennifer Stang

Introduction

Vegetarian For Life is a unique cookbook which reflects the peaceful Santa Barbara lifestyle. It is a collection of beautiful, main course, vegetarian, low-calorie, dairyless meals which are unusually colorful, appetizing, and filling. My cookbook also incorporates my special weight-loss diet plan for those who need help in losing weight pleasantly and permanently while eating healthy, vegetarian meals.

For three main groups of people: the dieter, the health-conscious, and the ill, Vegetarian For Life is designed to be a helpful resource. Dieters who have suffered through bizarre, self-destructive weight-loss regimes will find that my program provides a safe, balanced, efficient method for weight reduction. (Those seeking weight-loss should use my recipes in conjunction with my diet program and supplementary diet suggestions)

The health-conscious can also benefit from my book. With the onset and continuation of the health and exercise movement, people are becoming more aware of their bodies and the positive results from a pure diet. Since medical evidence has correlated our nation's leading health disorders to poor dietary habits (e.g., heart disease from high-cholesterol/high-fat foods, cancer from high-fat diets, etc.), people are seeking alternatives- practical and interesting ways to eat for health and longevity. A typical meat and potatoes diet no longer suffices, nor do new-fangled fad diets. Vegetarian For Life provides the concrete suggestions and guidance that lead to a lifetime of physical and mental well-being.

And finally, my book is designed to aid those suffering from physical pain, whose bodies are deteriorating from years of dietary abuse and imbalanced lifestyles. When the ill recognize that they must change their eating habits in order to heal, they often seek medical advice. Yet the medical establishment lacks solid, alternative, resource books to give their confused, floundering patients who must clean up their act. Vegetarian For Life is designed to instruct and provide guidance towards healing and strength.

You will find only main dish recipes in my book. One of the biggest challenges for cooks and dieters is to collect a recipe "crock-pot" of interesting, nutritional, primary courses to serve throughout the year-snacks and smaller meals are easier to create. Free your artistic bent to accessorize these main dishes with complementary, vegetarian touches.

All recipes have been carefully compiled to facilitate ease in preparation and pleasure in taste. Squash blossoms, an unusual ingredient in many pop recipes, sound fragrant and exotic. But where does one find them? Certainly not in the Santa Barbara stores I frequent. (Actually, I did spot one bright, orange blossom one day while running on a hillside road in Santa Barbara.) Fennel bulbs may be gourmet heaven when prepared from contemporary, fanciful, recipes. How frustrating for the chef, however, when the local markets are bereft of these bulbous beasts. Once, when determined to sample an unusual recipe, I literally had to climb the Santa Ynez Mountains to locate and uproot a feisty, wild fennel plant. Consequently, my recipes are practical and simple with accessible ingredients. (Where a few slightly unusual substances are included, I have suggested where they might be purchased.)

As you use recipes in Vegetarian For Life you will notice that most recipes indicate that they serve one person (i.e., one very hearty eater). If you are blessed with being a normal or small eater, the recipes should be plenty for two or more people.

Why Dairyless

The miraculous human body is intricate and baffling. How nice it would be if we were created with an operations and repair manual to inform us how to run and service our individual machines for perfect performance. Without instructions, however, we faithfully rely on parents (when we are little) and doctors to educate, treat, and heal us.

As they mature, and after experiencing various chronic physical problems, many people find that their family foods and traditional diets do not contribute to their maximum health, nor do the medical treatments alone prescribed by their doctors. These are difficult realizations; they require an analysis and breakdown of one's comfortable belief systems, as well as an acceptance of personal responsibility for one's own health. Yet by opening the mind, listening to the body, deciphering its specific signs and symptoms, and then moving forth with courage, one can learn to discern the good, effective health practices from the bad.

A commonly accepted dietary belief that I feel needs further examination is that dairy products are healthful and should be a part of the daily diet. As a teenager, I had a constant, general mucousy condition in my nose and throat, as well as frequent debilitating bouts of sore throats and tonsillitis. I was at the point of having a tonsillectomy. As a last resort, by recommendation of an insightful doctor, I discontinued drinking milk and eating dairy foods. This immediately eliminated my incessant sore throats and tonsillitis. Thankfully, I still have my god-given tonsils which help me fight naturally other diseases. After years of being told by doctors and teachers that dairy products comprise one of the basic food groups -which we must eat every day- and by parents that we must "finish our milk" with our meals, it is difficult to consider that dairy products might be deleterious to our health. Fortunately, a few new-age nutritionists and doctors are now presenting enlightening evidence which substantiates that dairy products are detrimental to the human body. Do you realize that we are the only animal that continues to ingest milk after weaning? Yes, cow's milk is a perfectly nutritional food- for calves, that is! As far as I am concerned, dairy foods are mucous-inducing and contribute to a myriad of health disorders. To visualize its effect on my body, I picture milk coating my internal vessels like it coats the sides of a drinking glass; I imagine the stringy clumps of cheese and grease that solidify on a cold pizza sitting and clotting in my tender stomach. This is graphic, but real. In his book. Survival Into the 21st Century, Viktoras Kulvinskas states that, "milk tends to form a large curd in the stomach which can take up to 48 hours to eliminate. Or, it can surround other foods with curd, isolating them from gastric juices." This stresses the body, which, in turn, can overstimulate and break down the immune system, allowing for various forms of cancer -such as Hodgkin's Disease-to occur.

In addition, allergies, arthritis, arterial degeneration, cataracts, respiratory problems, and many other degenerative diseases may be partly or wholly attributed to dairy food consumption. According to John A. McDougall, M.D. and Mary A. McDougall in their book, The McDougall Plan, dairy products are "high in fat, protein, and environmental contaminants and deficient in fiber and carbohydrates." Dairy products are the "leading source of food allergies." In other words, one need not have the all too common lactose intolerance to be adversely affected by dairy foods. This over-concentrated protein source harms the infant, the adolescent, and the adult.

To compound these problems, commercial milk is fortified with synthetic vitamin D2. This substance, which is alien to our bodies, can be a factor in kidney failure, mental retardation, dental abnormalities, and heart murmurs. Unlike natural vitamin D3 - which is produced by the body when exposed to sunlight- synthetic vitamin D2 fails to regulate the body's delicate calcium balance.

To eliminate dairy foods from the diet is to take a step towards vibrant health. Understandably, one might be concerned as to whether or not the proper vitamins and nutrients -such as calcium, protein, vitamin B12, vitamin D, and iron- can be obtained from this new diet. Yet, a well-planned, vegetarian, dairyless regime is by far more wholesome and clean than the typical American diet. It can easily contain all the necessary nutrients to build a strong, well-fortified body. A quote from the June, 1985 issue of "Runner's World" magazine states: "A vegan diet, in fact, requires less nutritional consciousness than a meat-based diet." Let's examine this further.

A major concern for aspiring vegetarians is how to get adequate calcium from non-meat, non-dairy sources. First, one must understand that the important consideration is not how much calcium is ingested, but rather its quality and ability to be absorbed. The McDougalls state that "the amount of calcium present in the diet has little effect on the quantity of calcium that is eventually taken into the body. The intestine absorbs from the foods consumed sufficient calcium to meet the needs of the body. On low-calcium diets, the efficiency of absorption is increased, and on high-calcium diets less absorption occurs." Furthermore, "calcium deficiency of dietary origin is a myth and is virtually unknown in humans, even though most people in the world do not consume milk after weaning."

Where can one get natural calcium? Good sources are: almonds, broccoli, dandelion greens, green, leafy vegetables, spinach, and walnuts.*

The most frequent question I am asked regarding my dairyless vegetarianism is, "How do I get enough protein?" In his book, The Pritikin Program, the late Nathan Pritikin summarizes and resolves the protein issue: "The body's need for protein has been grossly exaggerated... The best sources of protein are grains, roots, vegetables, and fruits in an unrefined, minimally processed form... All natural food grown contains all of the amino acids, 'essential' and 'non-essential', in sufficient quantities to satisfy human requirements." In fact, too much protein can cause a negative mineral balance, which means that the body actually loses important minerals such as calcium, iron, magnesium, phosphorus, and zinc. The McDougalls reiterate that excess "protein actually washes calcium from the body into the kidney system, leaving calcium-deficient bones and an increased risk of kidney stones." Like the strongest animals: the ox, elephant, horse, who maintain life on a diet of grasses, or the fruitarian gorilla, with whom we have an identical digestive system, humans can derive sufficient protein from a vegetarian, dairyless diet.

In addition, it is not necessary to eat foods that contain all of the essential amino acids in one meal. Viktoras Kulvinskas says, "most people maintain health and adequate protein intake from a mixed, varied diet. The deficiency of an essential amino acid in one protein in the diet can be supplemented by adding another protein which contains the missing amino acid... However, there is no need to eat a complete protein mixture at any one meal... Amino acids are in a continual state of flux from one part of the body to the other. If the amount of the amino acids in the cells of one area falls too low, then amino acids will enter these cells from the blood and will be replaced by amino acids released from other cells."

Some quality protein sources are: fruits, grains, nuts, roots, seeds, sprouts, and vegetables.*

What about vitamin B12? Previously thought to be contained in only animal-based foods, B12 is in fermented foods, sea vegetables, soybean foods, such as miso (a marvelously flavorful, complete-protein, soybean paste), tempeh, tamari, and spirulina algae.*

Finally, vitamin D and iron need not be obtained from milk or meat sources, either. Intermittent exposure to sunlight produces vitamin D and allows this fat-soluble vitamin to be stored in body fats for long periods of time. Additional intake of vitamin D is unnecessary. And iron is plentiful in beans, corn, green, leafy vegetables, and wheat- all normal constituents of a vegetarian diet.* In fact, ascorbic acid, most commonly found in the fruits and vegetables a vegetarian usually eats, enhances the body's ability to absorb iron.

So, let us leave milk to nourish the young calves for whom it was created, and stop hindering ourselves with unnatural substances. Let us allow our bodies the dignity to develop and function naturally for a lifetime of ultimate health and well-being.

For further information regarding the dangers of dairy products and alternative healthy ideas for mind and body I recommend the following literature:

Light Eating for Survival, by Marcia Madhuri Acciardo

Survival Into the 21st Century, by Viktoras KulvinskasThe

Book of Miso, by Akiko Aoyagi and William ShurtleffThe

Handbook to Higher Consciousness, by Ken Keyes, Jr.The McDougall Plan, by John A. McDougall, M.D. and Mary A. McDougall

The Pritikin Program for Diet and Exercise, by Nathan Pritikin with Patrick M. McGrady, Jr.

*These foods are used throughout my recipes

A History of the Vegetarian For Life Diet

For many people, the worst four letter word in the English language is F-O-O-D. "Diet" runs a close second- in fact, why not just drop the "T"?

From the moment of birth I have experienced a love-hate relationship with food, relishing its taste and ability to be a sensual source of warmth, comfort, and satisfaction in my life. As would be expected, I have been heavier than I would have ideally liked for most of my life. So, my task was to find an effective weight loss program where I would not sacrifice my health or my sanity. In my discouraging and painfully frustrating search for the perfect plan, I suffered through diets that were distastefully boring and unappetizing, or programs with microscopic portions, realistically designed for petite eaters. Then there were the regimes created for short-term use, after which time I gained back twice as much weight as I had lost. Worse were the diets based upon the use of unhealthy, non-nutritive foodstuffs, chemicals, and meat that were potentially injurious to my health. I knew there had to be a sane alternative. Vegetarianism beckoned.

Many people have the notion, like I did, that when one becomes a vegetarian he or she will automatically shed weight. For the normal eater this is frequently true since heavy, indigestible food is replaced by lighter vegetarian fare. This is rarely true, however, for the compulsive eater. The cessation of meat and dairy product consumption activates what I call the "chew response," that is- a craving to gnaw on chunky, chewy foods such as grains, natural sweets, and nuts. Consequently, the frustrated dieter gains weight, as he/she is driven to eat large quantities of highly caloric, vegetarian foods. After adding too many pounds, I realized I had to discover a method for trouble-eaters, like myself, to diet healthfully without feeling the anguish and painful repercussions of food deprivation.

After twelve years of vegetarianism, exhaustive research, and endless trouble-shooting, I have developed a marvelous system for losing/maintaining weight while feeling happy, healthy, and full- the Vegetarian For Life diet system. My simple, yet effective program includes using the repertoire of delectable, unique recipes in this book, as well as a few helpful hints that I gladly share with my readers.

May you reach your goals and experience the peace and fulfillment that I feel from this more balanced, disciplined way of life.

The Actual Diet

My program for weight loss and/or maintenance is really quite easy. After all, when one becomes aware of the body's needs and idiosyncrasies, a simple balance of calorie intake and expenditure will result in weight change. The Vegetarian For Life diet program has guided me, giving me the exhilarating feeling of control over my more impetuous side while I care for my whole self in a disciplined, reliable way. Here is how:

First, mentally prepare yourself to be your finest friend. At times, people and situations might deflate you. You, however, are the one ultimately in control of your feelings and reactions. Thus, you can always be self-supporting and positive. Deliberately surround yourself with kind people and lovely things. Decide to shape yourself and your life into the beautiful image of perfection that resides in your heart.

Start out fresh. Treat yourself to fine equipment for recording notes about your progress and the wonderful steps you are taking to improve your life. Buy yourself a large, lined pad of paper, an attractive folder for notes, and a pen with which you enjoy writing. In addition, purchase a thorough calorie counter book. (I find that Calories and Carbohydrates by Barbara Kraus and The Natural Foods Calorie Counter by Groves, Lissance, and Olsen are both very helpful resources.) Remember, everything you do, each action you take should be special. You are special and deserve the best.

Next, determine your objective. Do you want to lose weight or maintain it? Set a goal. Then figure out the amount of calories you want to consume to reach your goal.

For example, if you seek a thinner body, first you must calculate your daily caloric intake. The most accurate and individualized method for doing this is to complete a one week diet tally. More specifically, add up all the calories you consume in your average week, then divide the total by seven. This number represents your average daily caloric intake. To facilitate weight loss, decrease this number by 500 - 1,000. The result will be your new calorie number guide, (i.e. the maximum amount of calories you will consume in one day). Memorize it! By using this number as your guide you will ingest less calories each day, each week, each year, and you will lose weight.

To maintain your weight, simply multiply what you consider to be your ideal weight by twelve. The product will be your new calorie number guide. For example, if you weigh -and wish to continue weighing- 120 pounds, multiply 120 times twelve. The product, 1440, will be your daily calorie limit.

Whether you desire weight loss or maintenance, please be sure to be sensitive to your individual body and its needs as it changes; adjust your calories as necessary. Obviously, there are no exact rules that work for everyone. For example, if you are not losing weight as quickly as you would like, reduce your calorie number guide; if you are feeling truly weak or deprived, slightly increase your daily caloric intake and allow your body to reduce at a slower pace. Never rush weight loss. Trust yourself to modify your calories for maximum effectiveness of the diet.

Also, become aware of your body as it digests different foods. Do you digest some foods more easily than others? Do some foods hamper your digestion and feel like lead in your stomach? Be kind to yourself by avoiding anything that stresses, clogs, bloats or irritates your body. And most of all, be sure to take time to be proud of the new sensible control you exercise over your body.

I used 1,000 calories per day as my calorie number guide to lose weight. Now I use this same number to maintain my weight! Strangely enough, a 1,000 calorie limit initially helped me lose an undesired 50 extra pounds of weight. Now, however, it maintains my weight at a set point, (i.e. a natural, normal weight-stabilization point). By carefully observing my body's works, taking into account my height, weight, exercise habits and how I metabolize different foods, I arrived at a manageable and effective calorie number guide to help me reach my objectives.

In order to keep track of your calorie intake in a sane and organized way, from now on you will log in all foods consumed each day (except "free and easy" foods). When you reach your calorie number guide, that is, your limit for the day, STOP. Clearly, you will need some forethought so that you do not consume all calories allowed at breakfast, leaving none available for later. For instance, since dinner is my favorite meal of the day, I plan ahead. In the morning I select a dinner from my book for which I am especially in the mood. I jot down the number of calories it will use up, then plan my breakfast and light lunch accordingly. When planning, be strategic. Think carefully about your days-when are your weak or hard times? Save up calories for a treat to help you through those times. Be honest with yourself and take care of your needs.

Here is an example of my charting system:

Date	Food and Calories	Wt.	Notes
3/8 Mon	SALAD Hot Greek Apple Orange 1 T. Oil SALAD		
	90 80(170) 120(290) 651 = (941)	130	Peaceful; Clear skin
3/9 Tues.	1 Pt. 1 Rice Crkr Crispy Strawb. 1 T. Tahini Eggplt. Papaya		
	(122) 130 (252) 476(728) 100 = (828)		Upset Stomach
	Subtotal After Each Meal Total Calories For the Day		

Notice that I enter in the day and date, and each food I eat with the calories each contains. In parenthesis I keep a running subtotal of calories consumed after each meal or snack. Finally, I circle the total number of calories when I am either through eating for the day or have reached my 1,000 calorie limit. If absolutely necessary, allow yourself a little leeway over your limit, but not much. In other words, when desperate, I will allow myself additional calories up to -but never over- 1,099 (so that I am still in the 1,000 range). If you need to eat a tidbit more, first try to use items from the "free and easy" list. However, if "free and easy" foods just will not "cut the cake," follow the leeway system.

Rather than repeatedly looking up calories in a book, try jotting down the foods that you eat most often and their caloric contents on an index card. Tape the index card to your cupboard for a handy reference.

No one wants to be deprived of certain fun foods or excluded from the pleasures of normal dining. In fact, feelings of deprivation are frequently compensated for by bouts of binge eating. Be good to yourself. Internally accept that you can eat any food that you desire- of course, in moderation. Know that you deliberately choose to eat the foods you eat because they feel physically and psychically better to you. Morally, I will not eat animal flesh, fish, or fowl friends, but otherwise I try to trust and accept whatever my body asks for. At times it is difficult to allow myself the freedom to eat what I would normally consider "garbage" food. But through time and reconditioning I find that my unhealthy cravings are disappearing as I fill my mind and body with new, healthy substances and habits.

It is mandatory to keep track of your weight. I strongly suggest that you periodically weigh yourself; say, two times per week. Jot down your weight on your chart. If your objective is to lose weight, why not circle your losses with a brightly-colored pen? Celebrate! Never, however, weigh yourself if you are depressed or feeling bloated (perhaps from stress or menstruation, etc.). It will only make you feel more unhappy and unsuccessful. Respect your body's moods and fluctuations. Your happiness is much more important than your adherence to rigid rules.

Use the right hand section of your chart to note daily feelings, observed bodily changes and fresh ideas to inspire you.

Careful monitoring of your caloric intake, coupled with regular exercise and a positive disposition will result in weight control. Each scrumptious meal in Vegetarian For Life is light, with calories tallied for your convenience to assist you in reaching your goal.

Supplementary Diet Suggestions

Allow yourself ten minutes of peace or quiet meditation before your main meals. This will bring focus and calm to your appetite so that you can control exactly what and how much you want to eat.

Sip a glass of something refreshing before or while you prepare your meals. I prefer a frosty glass of carrot or tomato juice, or even cool distilled water, all mixed with a spoonful of liquid chlorophyll. Not only does chlorophyll cleanse and strengthen the blood cells, destroy putrefactive bacteria in the intestines, and re-establish natural bacteria flora which manufacture vitamin B12, but it will also soothe any hunger pangs.

Exercise regularly. When one diets, his/her metabolic rate drops to conserve energy, making it more difficult to lose weight. So, to facilitate weight loss, immerse yourself in one or more types of exercise that appeal to you. Your metabolism will regulate at a new high, burning your food faster and calming your appetite. And as you take pride in your stimulated body, a health-oriented momentum will guide you to desire and eat more wholesome and healthy food.

Be gentle and understanding with yourself. Try not to be self-critical. 'You will succeed. Any mistakes you make will simply provide opportunities for increased self-knowledge and growth.

For a light and nourishing snack, sip on carrot juice during the day. (I dilute it with distilled water, three parts" carrot juice to one part water). It is a wonderful source of vitamins A, B, C, D, E, and K as well as calcium, magnesium, iron, phosphorus, sulfur, silicon, and chlorine. In addition, its delicious.

Set an early evening hour after which you will not eat. I usually try to stop eating after 7:30 p.m., however I will allow myself tea and occasionally one piece of fruit, (i.e., if it fits into my calorie count for the day), or a "free and easy" vegetable later on in the evening. The most important point is not to let yourself feel deprived or frustrated; yet at the same time be careful not to eat as a diversion from emotional imbalances. If your habits or temperament require that you eat in the later evening or at unusual hours, by all means respect your needs. If you follow my program, you will still be successful. In the later hours, if you need a filling and satisfying treat, use the "free and easy" list of foods. Carrot juice, tomato juice (cold with a splash of lemon or simmered with a dash of parsley), vegetables, or even a light salad are some of my favorite snacks in desperate times.

If your goal is to lose weight, use a non-stick vegetable spray in lieu of oil whenever possible, (when frying, sauteing, baking, etc.) to cut down on calories. Although non-stick sprays are clearly not as healthy as fresh olive oil, they can be a useful tool in your weight-loss plan.

If possible, shop weekly for staples but daily for main meal ingredients at an inspiring health store. Rather than scrounging up a meal from undesirable foods at home, this shopping method allows you to be in touch with what you need to eat each day to feel physically and emotionally satisfied.

Keep busy. Involve yourself in healthful activities such as growing your own vegetables, herbs, sprouts, or wheat grass. Chewing on these healthy munchies is a wonderful way to occupy a hungry mouth.

Free and Easy Foods

The following foods can be eaten at anytime in any amount, unless otherwise specified, as part of the Vegetarian For Life diet program. Try to eat these foods in moderation. However, feel free to use them as your allies in tenuous times.

The asterisk * means free from calorie counting; the plus sign + means limitations apply.

+ <u>BROTH OR BOUILLON (vegetable only)</u>: I enjoy Jensen's broth powder or Vegex broth cubes. They are both delicious and nutritious. Note: limit yourself to 4 cups prepared broth or 4 cubes per day.

+ <u>CARBONATED WATER (unsweetened)</u>: splurge on Perrier, A Sante, Calistoga, Arrowhead etc.

+ <u>CARROT JUICE:</u> limit yourself to one pint pure carrot juice per day.

* <u>COFFEE:</u> I strongly recommend avoiding this toxic substance. However, if you feel the need to indulge, keep your consumption to a minimum.

* <u>EDIBLE FLOWERS AND LEAVES:</u> these make sensational accoutrements:

Chamomile

Pansy

Chives

Primrose

Chrysanthemum

Quince

Crab apple

Raspberry leaves

Elderberry

Rose petals

Fuchsia

Rose hips

Garlic

Rosemary

Geranium

Sage

Gladiolas

Sorrel

Grape leaves

Spearmint

Lavender

Squash flowers

Marigold

Strawberry leaves

Milkweed

Sweet potato flowers

Mulberry

Thyme

Nasturtium

Tiger lily pods

Violet

...and any other beauties

* HERBAL TEA: have fun trying the wide assortment of flavors. I particularly enjoy Celestial Seasonings' cinnamon rose and country apple teas or Lipton's cinnamon apple and orange spice teas.

* HERBS: our earth provides a bounty of tastes and varieties of herbs. Sample and experiment to your heart's content.

+ HONEY: use up to two tablespoons freely for breakfast and lunchtime hours. Count honey calories after lunch and through the evening hours.

* KELP AND SEAWEED: this includes dulse, hiziki, kelp powder, kombu, nori, wakame, etc. These tasty treats are full of iodine, rich minerals, and trace elements. They are low calorie and easy to digest when re-hydrated. Eat them plain, dry or soaked, and/or mixed in with a favorite dish. (Look for them in the oriental section of your supermarket.)

* LEMON JUICE: fresh is best.

* LIME JUICE: freshly squeezed if possible

* <u>MUSTARD:</u> prepared or dry.

* NON-STICK VEGETABLE SPRAY

* <u>PICKLES (dill, not sweet):</u> look for a nice variety in your health store that does not contain formaldehyde or chemicals. "Cosmic Cukes" are yummy crunchers.

* SAUERKRAUT

* TAMARI OR SOY SAUCE

* TOMATO JUICE OR VEGETABLE JUICE

* TOMATO PASTE. PUREE. OR SAUCE

VEGETABLES:

Alfalfa sprouts

Kale

Arugula

Kohlrabi

Artichoke

Lambs quarters (a vegetable green)

Asparagus

Leeks

Bamboo shoots

Lentil sprouts

Beets

Mint

Beet greens

Mung bean sprouts

Bok Choy

Mushrooms (all varieties)

Broccoli

Mustard greens

Bronze lettuce

Okra

Brussel sprouts

Onions

Butter lettuce

Parsley

Cabbage

Parsnips

Peas

Capers

Pimiento

Carrots

Raddichio

Cauliflower

Radishes Radish

Celery

sprouts

Chard

Chicory

Chili peppers

Chinese pea pods

Red clover sprouts

Chives

Red bell pepper

Collard greens

Romaine

Cucumber

Rutabagas

Dandelion

Scallions

Eggplant

Shallots

Endive

Sorrel

Escarole

Spinach

Fenugreek sprouts

Summer squash (all varieties)

Garlic

Sunchokes (Jerusalem artichokes)

Gherkins

Sunflower sprouts

Grasses

Tomatoes Turnips

Green beans

Turnip greens

Green bell pepper

Watercress Wax beans

Hearts of palm

Horseradish

Jalapeno peppers

Jicama

...you get the idea!

+ <u>Vegetables NOT ALLOWED In Unlimited Amounts:</u>
(Count calories of all these vegetables)

- Dry beans and peas: chick peas, kidney beans, lentils, limas, navy beans, pinto beans, split peas, soy beans, etc.

- Nuts: all varieties

- Pumpkin

- Starchy or fatty vegetables: avocado, corn, olives, potatoes, etc.

- Winter squashes: acorn, banana, butternut, calabaza, Des Moines, gold nugget, hubbard, peppercorn, table queen, Turk's turban, etc.

* <u>VINEGAR:</u> cider vinegar is the best to use.

* <u>WATER:</u> drink distilled water whenever possible.

Healthful Hints

<u>Cooked foods</u>: eat raw foods, rather than cooked foods, as frequently as possible. In the raw state, foods provide the maximum amount of nutrients for your body.

<u>Fasting</u>: fast periodically for one day or more to: detoxify your body, center your energy, and to give your digestive organs a rest.

<u>Food labels</u>: be aware of what you eat. Read labels carefully to avoid foods laden with chemicals, preservatives, dyes, and other artificial substances.

<u>Fresh foods</u>: always use pure, fresh, unrefined foods when available; avoid processed, canned products.

<u>Fruit juices</u>: when drinking fruit juice, dilute it with an equal amount of distilled water or natural carbonated water (to make a fruity soda treat). This will prevent an overload or "rush" of sugar into the blood stream.

<u>Grains</u>: buy only whole, unprocessed grains. During the refining process, grains lose much of their nutritive value. In their natural state, whole grains provide a variety of proteins, carbohydrates, vitamins, minerals, trace elements, and fiber.

<u>Liquids</u>: avoid drinking liquids with your meals: Liquids dilute the digestive juices, thus, disrupting the digestive process. Drink liquids one half hour before or one hour after meals.

<u>Molasses</u>: use unsulphured molasses to avoid ingesting sulphur. (Note: black strap molasses is a by-product, that is, a waste material from sugar refinery.)

<u>Oils</u>: the best oils to use are olive oil (it is easy to digest and rich in green chlorophyll), avocado oil, and sesame oil. Buy cold-pressed, unfiltered, virgin oil whenever possible. Also, keep oils refrigerated to prevent them from getting rancid.

<u>Salt</u>: limit salt intake; substitute broth powder or other herbal, vegetable seasonings for salt.

<u>Soy Sauce</u>: tamari is a pure soy sauce free from chemicals and preservatives. It has a rich, lusty flavor. Use it instead of commercial soy sauce.

<u>Sprouts</u>: garnish meals with fresh sprouts (e.g., alfalfa, adzuki, garbanzo, lentil, mung bean, radish, soybean, sunflower, etc.) or munch them for a healthy, low-calorie snack. They are bursting with vitamins and minerals, are high in protein and enzymes, and are easily digested.

<u>Steaming vegetables</u>: steam vegetables rather than boil them. Steaming helps retain the maximum amount of vitamins and nutrients. (If you do boil your vegetables, save the broth to use in soup.)

<u>Stimulants</u>: stimulants, (e.g., coffee, cigarettes, caffeine, spices, sugar, etc.) are hazardous and should be avoided. Substitute for them with natural herbs, sweeteners, and foods.

<u>Sugar</u>: avoid sugar and sugar substitutes, (e.g., white sugar, brown sugar, aspartame, saccharine, etc.). If you have a sweet tooth, use a touch of organic, unrefined, unfiltered honey -which contains trace minerals- or pure maple syrup.

<u>Thickening agents</u>: when in need of a thickening agent, use arrowroot or whole wheat flour instead of cornstarch.

These substitutes are healthier and are good protein sources.

<u>Vinegar</u>: use cider vinegar in lieu of white or wine vinegar whenever possible. Cider vinegar is made from naturally fermented apples. Other vinegars are usually distilled, with sugar and chemicals added.

<u>Water</u>: stick with distilled or naturally carbonated, spring water.

Recipes

Almost all of the following recipes have been designed for one big eater. It is very possible that the meals will be plenty for two people or more. Please use your discretion when preparing the recipes: adjust amounts and calories according to your true needs.

In keeping with my diet program, the tallies at the end of each recipe include only the caloric content of "limited" foods, as explained in the diet program. Calories in Free and Easy Foods chapter are not added in. All calories are listed per individual serving.

Artichoke Ensemble

1 1/3 c. distilled water

1/3 c. raw wild rice

1 bay leaf

non-stick vegetable spray

2 T. olive oil

1 sm. eggplant, cut in cubes

3/4 c. distilled water

10 mushrooms, halved

1 pt. cherry tomatoes, halved or 3 tomatoes, cut in wedges

1 can artichoke hearts (in water), drained

20 raw almonds, whole, halved, or slivered

1 T. dried parsley

1/2 t. garlic powder

1/3 t. salt (optional)

1/4 t. Thyme

Put 1 1/3 c. water in a medium saucepan. Bring to a boil then add rice and bay leaf. Reduce heat, cover and simmer for 30 minutes, or until rice is tender and water is absorbed.

While rice cooks, spray a large frying pan with nonstick spray. Begin to heat pan then add oil. Sauté eggplant until oil is absorbed. Stir in 3/4 c. water and mushrooms. Cover frying pan and simmer for 10 minutes or until eggplant is soft. Mix in tomatoes, artichoke hearts, almonds, parsley, garlic powder, salt, and thyme. Cover frying pan again and continue cooking for 5 more minutes. Serve Artichoke Ensemble topped with wild rice.

Serves 1

Calories:
wild rice - 188
oil - 240
almonds - 120
548 total

Avocado Cream Soup

1 avocado, pitted

1 1/4 c. distilled water

1 tomato, quartered

1 sm. lemon, juiced

t. cider vinegar

cubes or 2 t. vegetable bouillon

t. garlic powder

t. spirulina algae*

1/8-1/4 t. cayenne pepper

1 green bell pepper, seeded

2 scallions, chopped

1/2 t. basil

1 t. salt or tamari

1 c. fresh or frozen peas

8 oz. raw mushrooms, sliced

2 c. raw broccoli, chopped

fresh parsley and/or watercress

In a blender, combine avocado, water, tomato, lemon juice, vinegar, bouillon, garlic, algae, cayenne, bell pepper, scallions, basil, and salt. Blend until smooth.

Pour blended vegetables into a saucepan. Stir in peas, mushrooms and broccoli. Bring soup to a boil, then lower heat and simmer, uncovered, for 10 minutes, or until vegetables are tender. Garnish avocado cream soup with fresh parsley or watercress, if desired.

Serves 1

Calories:

avocado - 369
algae - 55
421 total

*Powdered, nutritional algae available in health food stores.

Avocado Dream Boats

3 lg. zucchini, halved lengthwise

1 avocado, mashed

1 T. lemon juice

1 t. cider vinegar

1 T. fresh cilantro, chopped

1 green onion, minced

2 stalks celery, finely chopped

1/2 t. salt (optional)

1/2 t. garlic powder

1 t. dry vegetable broth

paprika

1 T. raw sunflower seeds lemon wedges

Steam zucchini for about 8 minutes or until crisp-tender. Put under cool water until handleable. With a spoon, scrape out pulp, being careful not to tear zucchini skin. Put pulp into a strainer and press out moisture.

In a mixing bowl combine pulp, avocado, lemon juice, vinegar, cilantro, onion, celery, salt, garlic, and broth. Mix well.

Place zucchini "boats" on a serving platter. Stuff with avocado mixture. Sprinkle with paprika and top with sunflower seeds. Serve with a garnish of lemon wedges.

Serves 1

Calories:
avocado - 370
sunflower seeds - 51
421 total

Broccoli Rolls Amandine

1 bunch broccoli

4 med. tomatoes, cut in wedges

12 oz. silken tofu or 7 oz. reg. tofu

1 T. miso*

3 T. fresh lemon juice

1 t. honey

1 T. dill weed

few dashes cayenne pepper

tamari, to taste (optional)

6 sheets nori seaweed**

20 almonds, slivered sunflower sprouts (or any available green sprout)

Cut stalks off broccoli, leaving 2 1/2 inch stems. In a large saucepan, steam broccoli for 8 minutes. Add tomatoes; steam for 5 to 8 more minutes or until broccoli is tender. Drain vegetables well; separate tomatoes from broccoli.

Make sauce: blend tofu, miso, lemon juice, honey, dill, cayenne, and tamari (if desired) until creamy.

To make rolls: lay two sheets of nori at a time on a dry surface. Working quickly, place a bunch (1/6) of broccoli and tomatoes diagonally in the center or each nori sheet. Roll up nori diagonally. (i.e. from one lengthwise corner to the opposite end.) Repeat process with all nori sheets, using up all broccoli and tomatoes.

Place broccoli rolls on a serving platter, seam side down. Pout tofu sauce over rolls down the center; sprinkle with almonds. Garnish broccoli rolls amandine with sprouts.

Serves 1

Calories:
tofu - 170
miso - 35
honey - 22
almonds - 120
347 total

*Soybean paste available in oriental or health food stores.

**Pressed seaweed available in oriental or health food stores.

Brussel Beauties In Grape Sauce

1 lb. brussel sprouts, hard ends trimmed

2 carrots, diagonally sliced

25 pearl onions, outer skins removed

7 oz. (1/2 pkg.) tofu, cut in cubes

1 T. olive oil

1/2 c. orange juice

1 t. honey

1/4 t. salt (optional)

1/8 t. black pepper

1.4 t. garlic powder

2 dashes ginger

2 dashes dry mustard

1 T. arrowroot, mixed with a little water to make a paste*

1 c. seedless green grapes, halved

Steam brussel sprouts, carrots, and pearl onions until tender, (about 15-20 minutes). Add tofu to steamer, cover pan, and turn off heat.

Make grape sauce: heat oil in a small saucepan. Add orange juice, honey, salt, pepper, garlic powder, ginger, and mustard. Turn heat to medium-low; slowly stir in arrowroot paste, mixing until sauce is thick and smooth. Add grapes; mix well.

Put brussel sprout mixture in a serving dish. Smother with grape sauce.

Serves 1

Calories:
tofu - 170

oil - 120
orange juice - 60
honey - 22
arrowroot   - 29
grapes - 102
503 total

*A natural substitute for cornstarch is found in health.

Cabbage Patch Salad

1 med. green cabbage, cored

5 lg. sunchokes (Jerusalem artichokes), sliced

3/4 c. fresh or frozen peas

1 green or red bell pepper, diced

1 scallion, chopped

1 stalk celery, chopped

1 carrot, grated

1 zucchini, grated

1/2 pkg. (7 oz.) soft tofu, mashed

2 t. lemon juice

1 1/2 t. cider vinegar

1/2 t. tamari

1/4 t. dry mustard

1/4 t. tarragon

1/2 t. salt (optional)

1/8 t. black pepper

1 dill pickle, chopped

1 T. fresh parsley, chopped

1/4 t. horseradish

1 t. capers

1 t. caraway seeds

1 T. raw sunflower seeds

1 tomato, sliced in wedges

Steam cabbage and sunchokes for 25 to 30 minutes or until cabbage is tender. Remove sunchokes and mash; drain cabbage in colander.

Meanwhile, steam peas, bell pepper, scallion, celery, carrot, and zucchini for 20 minutes. Set aside.

In a large mixing bowl, combine tofu, lemon juice, vinegar, tamari, mustard, tarragon, salt, pepper, pickle, parsley, horseradish, capers, and caraway seeds. Mix well. Add sunchokes and steamed vegetables.

Place cabbage on a serving plate. Remove inner leaves to form a "bowl." Stuff with vegetable mixture. Sprinkle with sunflower seeds and garnish with tomato wedges. (For a lovely flower effect, try placing the tomatoes with the wedge edges in a circle around the vegetable filling.) Serve warm or chilled.

Serves 1

Calories:
tofu - 170
sunflower seeds - 45
215 total

Serving Suggestions: Serve with a piece of matzoh bread or a favorite cracker. (Be sure to count bread or cracker calories.)

Cabbage Wrapped Tempeh
With Spicy Dijon Sauce

4 sm. fresh beets, greens removed

1 med. head green cabbage, cored

7 oz. tempeh or pressed tofu(2 patties)*

2 sm. tomatoes, cut into 4 slices each

Spicy Dijon Sauce

1 sm. onion, finely chopped

1/4 c. Dijon mustard

3 T. honey

2 T. tamari

1 T. red wine vinegar

2 t. dried rosemary leaves

1 t. ginger powder

3/4 t. black pepper

Preheat oven to 400 degrees.

Steam beets 15 minutes in a large steamer; add cabbage and steam for 15 more minutes or until beets are tender and cabbage leaves are soft but still hold form. Peel off 8 large leaves, pat dry and lay flat on counter.

Run beets under cold water to remove outer skin. Slice each beet into 4 slices. Slice tempeh patties in half to make 4 thin rounds; cut each round in half to make a total 8 semicircle.

To assemble cabbage wraps, place 1 semi-circle tempeh at base (stem area) of cabbage leaf. Top with a tomato slice, then 2 beet slices. Fold sides of leaves over filling; roll up leaf starting at base. Repeat with remaining seven cabbage leaves. Place cabbage packages in 8"x 8" baking dish.

In a small bowl mix sauce ingredients. Pour sauce over cabbage and bake 20 minutes.

Serves 1
Calories:
tempeh - 300
honey - 192
492 total

*Soy patties found in health food stores.

Carrot Tart With Broccoli Shell Salad

4 lg. carrots, sliced

2 eggs, beaten

pinch nutmeg

salt and pepper to taste

non-stick vegetable spray

1/2 lb. (2 1/2 c.) broccoli, steamed for 10 minutes

2 oz. sm. shell pasta, cooked al dente, drained

2 lg. tomatoes, chopped

2 green onions, chopped

1/4 pkg. (3.5 oz.) tofu, cut in small pieces

3 T. fresh parsley, chopped

1 T. olive oil

1 T. red wine vinegar

1/2 t. salt (optional)

1/4 t. black pepper

1/2 t. garlic powder

1 t. basil

8 ripe black olives, sliced

Preheat oven to 400 degrees.

Steam carrots 20 minutes, or until very soft; mash. Add eggs, nutmeg, salt, and pepper to carrots, mixing thoroughly. Spray a 9 1/2" tart pan with non-stick spray. Pat carrot mixture on bottom and up sides of tart pan to form a crust. Place tart pan in a pan of hot water; bake 15 minutes. Cool at least 5 minutes (or overnight if desired).

While tart crust bakes mix remaining ingredients except olives. Let broccoli salad sit at least 5 minutes so flavors can blend. Fill cooled crust with broccoli shell salad. Decorate with sliced olives.

Serves 1

Calories:
eggs - 160
pasta - 210
tofu - 85
oil - 120
olives - 40
615 total

Variations:

~Add sliced or chopped red bell pepper and/or artichoke hearts (in water, not oil) to salad.

~To reduce calories omit tofu or pasta.

Chewy Vegetable Loaf

1 1/2 c. distilled water

1/2 c. raw whole grain flakes (e.g. barley, oats, wheat, etc.)

2 tomatoes, finely chopped

12 oz. tomato paste

2 T. honey

non-stick vegetable spray

1/2 lb. mushrooms, chopped

3 stalks celery, thinly sliced

2 green onions, chopped

1 egg, beaten

1/4 c. raw wheat germ

2 T. fresh parsley, chopped or 1 T. dried

1/4 t. black pepper

1 t. salt (optional)

1 T. tamari

3/4 t. dry mustard

1/2 t. thyme

1 t. garlic powder

Preheat oven to 450 degrees.

In a medium-sized saucepan bring water to a boil. Add flakes, cover, and cook over medium-low heat until water is absorbed (about 15 minutes.)

Meanwhile, make sauce: mix tomatoes, tomato paste, and honey. Set sauce aside.

Spray a loaf pan with non-stick spray. Mix cooked flakes with remaining ingredients. Put one-half of grain/ vegetable mixture into loaf pan. Top with one-half of the sauce. Pat in remaining grain/vegetable mixture and top with remaining sauce. Garnish with tomato slices, if desired. Bake for 40 – 50 minutes until firm.

Serves 1

Calories:
Flakes: 200 approximately (*check below for exact amt.)
egg - 80
wheat germ   - 92
honey - 128
500 total

*1/2 c. raw:
barley flakes - 200 calories
oat flakes   - 156 calories
rice flakes - 128 calories
wheat flakes - 210 calories

Chock Full of Mushrooms and Matzoh Ball Soup

Soup

non-stick vegetable spray

1 t. olive oil

3 green onions, chopped

1/2 lb. mushrooms, halved

1 stalk celery, thinly sliced

carrots, julienned

c. prepared vegetable broth

1 bay leaf

1/4 t. garlic powder

2-3 dashes cayenne pepper

lg. handful of sunflower sprouts, {or any other green sprout)

Matzoh Balls

2 eggs, separated

pinch cream of tartar

1/8 t. salt (optional)

1/2 c. matzoh meal

2 T. fresh parsley, chopped or 1 T. dried parsley

1/8 t. salt (optional)

1/8 t. black pepper

1/8 t. ground ginger

1/8 t. ground nutmeg

Spray a medium saucepan with non-stick spray. Begin to heat pan, then add oil. Sauté green onions until soft, (about 5 minutes.) Add rest of soup ingredients except, sprouts, cover pan and bring soup to a boil. Then lower heat and simmer.

Meanwhile, make matzoh balls: beat egg whites with cream of tartar until peaks are stiff, but not dry. In a separate bowl, beat yolks with 1/8 t. salt. Fold whites into yolks. Slowly mix in matzoh meal, parsley, and rest of seasonings. Mix well; set aside for 5 minutes.

Shape matzoh mix into 8 balls. Uncover soup; drop matzoh balls into soup, one by one. Cover soup and simmer for 15 minutes. (Balls will expand when cooking.) Turn off heat and gently stir in sprouts. Re-cover pan and let sit for 5 minutes to soften sprouts.

Serves 1

Calories:
oil - 40
eggs - 160
matzoh meals - 220
420 total

Chunky Chili

non-stick vegetable spray

1 T. olive oil

1 lg. onion, chopped

1 green bell pepper, cut in small chunks

1/2 lb. mushrooms, sliced

lg. stalks celery, sliced

1 t. garlic powder

lg. tomatoes, cut in wedges

1/2 c. distilled water

1/2 t. salt (optional)

2 t. chill powder

1 t. cumin

1/2 t. thyme

1/2 t. oregano

1 1/2 c. cooked pinto beans;(soy beans or kidney beans are O.K., too)

Spray a large frying pan with non-stick spray. Begin to heat pan, then add oil. Sauté onion, green pepper, mushrooms and celery with garlic powder until slightly tender. Add the rest of ingredients. Cover and simmer for 10-15 minutes or until vegetables are soft and flavors are blended. (Add more water if necessary. Or, if chili is too thin, stir in 1 T. arrowroot* mixed with cold water - to form a paste. Be sure to add in arrowroot's 29 calories.)

Serves 1
Calories:
oil - 120
pinto beans - <u>255</u>
375 total

Serving Suggestions:

~Serve with a fresh green salad.

~Garnish with sliced avocado and sprouts. (Be sure to count avocado calories.)

*A natural substitute for cornstarch available in health food stores.

Crispy Eggplant Slices With Barbecue Sauce

non-stick vegetable spray

3 eggs, beaten

1 very lg. eggplant, sliced widthwise 1/4" thick

salt (optional)

black pepper

lettuce leaves {butter lettuce, bronze, etc.)

1 lg. tomato, sliced

fresh or frozen peas, steamed

Barbecue Sauce

1/4 c. ketchup, (a brand made with honey preferably)

1/4 c. molasses

1 t. prepared mustard

1/2 t. garlic powder

1 t. Tamari

Preheat oven to 500 degrees.

Spray a baking sheet and a large frying pan with non-stick spray. Heat the frying pan. Dip the eggplant slices in egg, a few pieces at a time, then fry on both sides, over medium-high heat, until slightly browned, (about 2 minutes each side). Repeat procedure until all pieces is browned, spraying frying pan with non-stick spray in between each batch. Place fried slices on baking sheet; do not overlap. Bake 20-25 minutes or until skin is crispy and centers are tender.

While eggplant bakes, make sauce: mix all sauce ingredients in a saucepan. Bring to a boil, then keep warm over low heat until eggplant is done.

To serve, place eggplant slices on a large platter of lettuce leaves. Drizzle with barbecue sauce. Accompany with tomato slices and peas.

Serves 1

Calories:
3 eggs - 240
ketchup - 64
molasses - 172
476 Total

Variations:

~Instead of serving with raw tomato slices, cut tomatoes in half and bake them along with the eggplant. Drizzle with barbecue sauce, too, and enjoy.

Crunchy Vegetables in Tahini Sauce

Crunchy Vegetables

alfalfa sprouts and/or any other sprouts (e.g. buck wheat, radish, sunflower, etc.)

10 mushrooms, halved

2 stalks celery, sliced

2 tomatoes, sliced in wedges

1 lg. handful hiziki or arame seaweed, soaked 15 minutes in warm water*

Tahini Sauce

4 tomatoes, halved

1/2 lemons, juiced

T. raw tahini**

1/2 t. vegetable broth powder

2 dashes cayenne pepper

1 t. garlic powder

kelp powder, to taste (optional)***

Lay a nest of sprouts in a large, shallow bowl. Top with all other vegetables except seaweed.

Put sauce ingredients in a blender; blend until smooth and creamy. (If sauce is too thin, add more tahini - count calories; if sauce is too thick, add more lemon juice, another tomato, or distilled water.) Pour sauce over vegetables.

Put seaweed in a fine strainer; rinse very well and drain. Mound or sprinkle seaweed on top of sauce.

Serves 1

Calories:
tahini - 190

190 total

Variations:

~Add any favorite vegetables to this dish. Peas, jicama, watercress or any fresh choice would be delicious.

*Available in oriental or health food stores.

**Ground sesame seeds available in health food stores.

***Ground seaweed (kelp) found in health food stores.

Cucumber Boats á l'orange

3 cucumbers, peeled

non-stick vegetable spray

1/2 c. matzoh meal

1/2 c. distilled water

2 eggs beaten

1 stalk celery, chopped

sm. onion, chopped

sunchokes (Jerusalem artichokes) or 1 more stalk celery, chopped

1/4 t. ginger

1/4 t. black pepper

1 t. salt (optional)

1 T. dried parsley

Orange Sauce

1 T. olive oil

1 T. whole wheat flour

1/2 c. orange juice

1/4 t. salt (optional)

1/4 t. black pepper

1 t. honey

finely grated orange rind

Preheat oven to 400 degrees.

Cut cucumbers in half lengthwise; scoop out seeds, (reserving seeds), to form "boats." Spray a large baking pan with non-stick spray. Place boats in pan.

Mix matzoh meal with water until smooth. Beat in eggs. Add rest of ingredients, including reserved cucumber seeds. Stuff cucumbers with matzoh mix. Bake 35 minutes.

When cucumbers are done, make sauce. Heat oil in a small saucepan. Stir in flour over medium-low heat until blended. Slowly add orange juice. Mix in salt, pepper, and honey. Sauce should be smooth and creamy. Pour over cucumber boats. Sprinkle boats with orange rind.

Serves 1

Calories:
matzoh meal - 220
eggs - 160
oil - 120
flour - 25
orange juice - 60
honey - 22
607 total

Eggplant Enchiladas With Fiesta Rice

Fiesta Rice

1/4 c. raw wild rice

1 green onion, chopped

c. water

T. pimiento, chopped

1/4 t. salt (optional)

2 dashes black pepper

Sauce

8 oz. tomato sauce

6 oz. tomato paste

4 sm. tomatoes chopped

1/2 c. vegetable broth

2 t. garlic powder

2 green onions

1 t. cumin

1/4 t. dry mustard

1/4 t. cayenne pepper

1 t. salt {optional)

Enchiladas

1 lg. eggplant, cut lengthwise in 1/8" slices non-stick vegetable spray

1 T. olive oil

med. onion, chopped

t. garlic powder

1/2 lb. mushrooms, sliced

1/2 pkg. (7 oz.) tofu, chopped

20 black olives, sliced

1/2 t. salt (optional)

1 bunch fresh spinach, chopped

Preheat oven to 400 degrees.

Make rice: put rice, green onion, and water in medium saucepan. Bring to a boil, lower heat, cover, and simmer about 40 minutes. Stir in pimiento, salt, and pepper. Cover and cook 5 more minutes, or until water is absorbed.

Meanwhile, make sauce: put all ingredients in medium saucepan. Bring to a boil, lower heat, and simmer, uncovered, 30 minutes, or until thick; stir frequently.

In a large saucepan, steam eggplant slices for 10 minutes or until tender but still hold shape. Pat dry; set aside.

Spray large frying pan with non-stick spray. Begin to heat, then add oil. Sauté onion with garlic powder until tender. Add rest of enchilada ingredients, except spinach, and sauté 10 minutes, or until tender. Add spinach, cook and stir 5 more minutes. Drain mixture well.

To assemble: spray an 8"x 8" baking pan with non-stick spray. Lay out slices of eggplant. Put a generous amount of filling at large end of slices, roll up, and place in baking pan, seam side down. Cover enchiladas with sauce. Bake for 30 minutes.

To serve: make a bed of fiesta rice on a festive serving plate. Top rice with saucey enchiladas. Garnish with fresh parsley or fresh chopped green onion.

Serves 1

Calories:
rice - 142
oil - 120

tofu - 170
olives - 100
532 total

Egg rolls With Sweet and Spicy Mustard Sauce

Eggrolls

1 14 oz. pkg. fresh chop suey mixed vegetables

1/2 lb. mushrooms, sliced

1/3 lb. fresh bean sprouts

1/2 c. distilled water

11 eggroll wrappers

water

non-stick vegetable spray

Mustard Sauce

1/4 t. garlic powder

2 dashes ginger powder

1 T. honey

1 1/2 T. tamari

1 T. cider vinegar

1 T. ketchup (a brand made with honey, if possible)

1 T. distilled water

1/2 t. dry mustard

Preheat oven to 450 degrees.

In a large frying pan combine chop suey, mushrooms, bean sprouts, and 1/2 c. water. Bring to a boil, then lower heat to medium-low and cook, covered, for 10 minutes, or until vegetables are tender. Drain vegetables in a colander.

Lay out 6 egg roll wrappers. Place a generous amount of vegetables on one end of each wrapper; moisten opposite end of wrapper with water. Roll up each egg roll, beginning at vegetable side, sealing at moistened end. Repeat process until all wrappers and vegetables are used.

Spray a baking sheet with non-stick spray. Place egg rolls on baking sheet; bake 10 minutes. Remove egg rolls from oven, spray egg rolls with spray, then bake 10 more minutes, or until crispy-brown.

While egg rolls bake, mix all sauce ingredients.

Serve egg rolls on a platter with a bowl of sweet and spicy mustard sauce on the side.

Serves 1

Calories:
eggroll wrappers - 440
honey - 64
ketchup - 16
520 total

Esprit d' Eggplant

non-stick vegetable spray

2 lg. eggplants (about 3 lbs total), halved lengthwise

2 T. olive oil

2 lg. stalks celery, finely diced

1 lg. onion, finely chopped

5 tomatoes, diced

bay leaf

dashes thyme

1/2 t. salt (optional)

1/4 t. black pepper

T. fresh cilantro, chopped

T. capers

1/2 T. honey

T. lemon juice

Preheat oven to 400 degrees.

Spray a baking sheet with non-stick spray. Place eggplants, cut sides down, on sheet. Bake 30 minutes until soft. Peel eggplants, put pulp in a large mixing bowl and mash.

While eggplant is baking, spray a large frying pan with non-stick spray. Begin to heat pan, then add oil. Sauté celery and onion for 5-8 minutes until tender-crisp. Add tomatoes, bay leaf, thyme, salt, and pepper. Simmer, uncovered for 8-10 minutes until vegetables are very tender and flavors are blended; stir occasionally. Remove bay leaf.

Add tomato mixture to eggplant; stir in cilantro, capers, honey, and lemon juice. Mix well.

Serve hot or cold.

Serves 2

Calories per serving:
olive oil   - 120
honey - 48
168 total

Serving suggestions:

~Serve esprit on a fresh bed of butter lettuce, watercress, or sprouts with a side baked potato.

~Use esprit as a dip or topping for crunchy, baked tortilla chips, warm pita bread, or matzoh.

~Garnish esprit with sprinkles of fresh parsley, sliced green olives with pimiento, or Greek olives. (Count calories of any added "limited" foods.)

French Fennel Soup

4 scallions, chopped

2 carrots, thinly sliced

2 tomatoes, chopped

10 mushrooms, sliced

1 15 oz. can (1 1/2 c. cooked) garbanzo beans drained

1 head bronze lettuce, torn into pieces

1/2 c. distilled water

3/4 t. garlic powder

1/2 t. salt (optional)

3 dashes black pepper

2 dashes cayenne pepper

1 t. fennel (anise seed)

1 t. dried sage

Put all ingredients into a medium-sized saucepan. Bring to a boil, cover, lower heat and simmer 30 minutes. Remove from heat. Puree one-half of vegetables in blender with a little soup broth. Return pureed mix to saucepan; mix well.

Serves 1

Calories:
garbanzo beans - 507
507 total

Fruit Spice Vegetable Curry

non-stick vegetable spray
1 T. olive oil
1 med. onion, chopped
1/2 c. split peas (green or yellow)
1 T. curry
1 t. cumin
1 t. garlic powder
1 eggplant (about 1 lb.), cubed
1 sm. cauliflower, cut into flowerettes
3 1/4 c. distilled water
1 lemon, juiced
1 t. salt (optional)
1/4 t. black or white pepper
1/4 c. fresh parsley, chopped
1/4 c. shredded coconut
1/4 c. raisins, soaked in hot
water 20 minutes, drained

Spray a large frying pan with non-stick spray. Begin to heat pan then add oil. Sauté onion until tender and browned. Stir in split peas, curry, cumin, and garlic powder. Mix well. Add eggplant, cauliflower, and water. Bring to a boil. Cover pan, reduce heat, and simmer for 30 minutes, or until vegetables and peas are tender and water is absorbed. (Add more water to vegetables if necessary.) Turn off heat; stir in remaining ingredients until flavors are blended.

Serves 1

Calories:

oil - 120
split peas - 348
coconut - 185
raisins - 113
766 total

Serving Suggestions:

~Serve Fruit Spice Vegetable Curry in a large, tropical, wooden bowl. Top with fresh steamed spinach or raw watercress and sliced tomatoes.

Garden Minestrone

1/4 c. dry kidney beans

1/4 c. dry garbanzo beans{chick peas)

water

1 bunch fresh spinach, chopped or 1 pkg. frozen spinach, thawed

1 sm. zucchini, sliced

10 mushrooms, sliced

1 lg. stalk celery, sliced

1 lg. carrot, sliced

1 lg. tomato, chopped

1 c. distilled water

1 6 oz. can tomato paste

1 1/2 t. garlic powder

1/2 t. basil

1 t. salt (optional)

3 dashes black pepper

1/4 c. fresh parsley, chopped or 2 T. dried parsley

2 oz. pasta (e.g. macaroni, egg twists, or any other fun shape)

Cover kidney beans and garbanzos with water in a medium-sized saucepan. Bring to a boil, lower heat, cover and simmer for 1 hour and 15 minutes, or until beans are almost fully tender. Drain beans; rinse. Put beans and remaining ingredients back into saucepan. Cover pan and simmer for 30 more minutes.

Serves 1

Calories:
kidney beans - 159

garbanzos   - 180
macaroni - 210
549 total

Gaviota Gazpacho With Crispy Chips

non-stick vegetable spray

1 lg. zucchini or golden squash, cut in 1/2 widthwise and sliced thinly lengthwise

6 sm. corn tortillas, cut in eighths (wedges)

salt (optional)

2 c. tomato juice, chilled

1 sm. cucumber, cut in chunks

1 sm. green bell pepper, seeded, cut in chunks

2 tomatoes, cut in chunks

1 green onion, chopped

1/8 c. fresh parsley, chopped

3 oz. alfalfa sprouts

1/2 t. Horseradish

1/2 lemon, juiced

1/2 lime, juiced or 1/2 extra lemon, juiced

1/2 t. each: basil, garlic powder, tarragon, thyme pinch cumin

1 t. Paprika

Preheat oven to broil. Put oven rack as high as possible. Spray a baking sheet with non-stick spray. Lay out zucchini slices in a single layer. Broil for 10 minutes. Turn slices over. Set oven to 450 degrees.

Spray a large baking pan with non-stick spray. Lay out tortilla wedges. Sprinkle with salt, if desired. Bake until browned and crisp (about 20 minutes), stirring occasionally. (Leave zucchini slices in oven on high rack while tortilla wedges bake.)

Meanwhile, make gazpacho: put remaining ingredients in a food processor or blender. In pulses, blend until mixed, but still thick and slightly chunky. Pour gazpacho into a large glass serving bowl. Serve gazpacho as a dip or cold soup with zucchini and tortilla chips.

Serves 1

Calories:
tortilla chips - 360
360 total

Variations:

~Try gazpacho topped with: sliced black olives, chopped green chiles, hard-boiled egg, croutons, or any other creative addition. (Be sure to count extra calories.)

Herbed Mushrooms and Tomatoes

non-stick vegetable spray

1 T. olive oil

2 bay leaves

1 t. garlic powder

1 med. yellow onion, chopped

1 T whole wheat flour

1/2 c.liquid vegetable broth

3/4 c. tomato juice

2 med. tomatoes, chopped

3/4 lb. mushrooms, whole

1/2 t. thyme

1 lg. white onion, quartered

handful fresh parsley, chopped or generous sprinkle dry parsley

salt to taste

few dashes black pepper

3 oz. (about 35) ripe green olives, whole and pitted

Spray a medium-sized saucepan with non-stick spray. Begin to heat, then add oil. Sauté bay leaves, garlic, and yellow onion until onion is golden. Stir in flour and lower heat. Cook for a few minutes, stirring constantly, until mix is very thick (almost crumbly). Add broth, tomato juice, and tomatoes. (For a thinner or thicker mixture, adjust the amount of tomato juice added.) Stir well; bring to a boil. Add mushrooms, thyme, white onion, parsley, salt, and pepper. Adjust seasonings to taste. Simmer over medium-low heat, uncovered, for about 20 minutes, or until liquid is reduced and vegetables are tender. Stir in whole olives.

Serves 1

Calories:
oil - 120
flour - 25
olives - 125
270 total

Serving Suggestions:

~Accompany herbed mushrooms with a steamy baked potato or a favorite bread or cracker. (Be sure to count potato, bread, or cracker calories.)

Hiziki Salad With Tahini Ginger Dressing

Vegetables

1/2 c. hiziki seaweed*

8 dried shitake mushrooms (oriental mushrooms)

3 c. hot water

2 T. tamari

1/4 c. cider vinegar

1 head butter lettuce, torn

1/2 bunch watercress

1 c. (heaping) sunflower sprouts

1 c. (heaping) alfalfa sprouts

3 lg. radishes, sliced

a few fresh mushrooms, sliced

Tahini Ginger Dressing

1/4 c. raw tahini**

1 T tamari

3 1/2 T. distilled water

2 T. lemon juice

1 t. honey

1 t. fresh ginger root, peeled and grated

1/2 t. garlic powder

Soak hiziki and shitake mushrooms in 2 cups hot water for 30 minutes. Rinse well, then place in a small saucepan , with remaining 1 cup water, tamari and vinegar. Bring to a boil, cover and simmer for 15 minutes. Drain and cool. Slice mushrooms, if desired.

Make dressing: mix tahini and tamari until smooth. Slowly add water and lemon juice, blending until creamy. Stir in honey, ginger, and garlic.

To assemble, mix lettuce, watercress, both sprouts, radishes, and fresh mushrooms in a large salad bowl. Add dressing and toss, mixing all ingredients and breaking up sprouts. Top with hiziki mix.

Serves 1

Calories:
tahini - 380
honey - 22
402 total

Variations:

~Feel free to add fresh snow peas, thinly sliced carrots, or any other delicious vegetable to this heavenly salad.

*Found in oriental or health food stores.

**Ground sesame seeds found in health food stores.

Hot Greek Salad

1/4 c. dry white beans

2 c. water

2 bay leaves

1 1/4 lb. fresh green beans, trimmed and halved

1/2 lb. mushrooms, sliced

1 lg. onion, thinly sliced

1/2 c. cooked garbanzo beans (chick peas), drained

3 med. tomatoes, chopped

10 black Greek olives

1 1/2 T. basil

2 sm. lemons, juiced

salt to taste (optional)

black pepper to taste

2 T. olive oil

In a medium saucepan combine white beans, water, and bay leaves. Bring to a boil, then lower heat, cover and simmer 1 1/4 hours, or until beans are tender. Drain beans and discard bay leaves. (Beans can be cooked ahead of time.)

In a large saucepan, steam green beans, mushrooms, and onion 10-15 minutes, or until crispy-tender.

In a large mixing bowl toss white beans, steamed vegetables, garbanzos, tomatoes, olives, and basil. In a small bowl mix lemon juice, salt, and pepper; whisk in olive oil. Pour lemon-oil dressing over hot Greek salad; toss well.

Serves 1

Calories:

white beans - 153
garbanzos   - 169
olives - 89
240 total

Variations:

~To cut preparation time, omit white beans and replace

with another 1/2 c. cooked garbanzo beans.

~To reduce calories, omit white or garbanzo beans

Kelp Burritos I

Burritos

3-4 c. fresh or frozen peas

2 med. tomatoes, chopped

1 bunch watercress or 6 leaves bronze lettuce, shredded

6 sheets nori*

Water (to soften nori)

Lemon Tahini Sauce

4 T. raw tahini **

1/4 c. lemon juice

1/2 t. garlic powder

1/2 c. distilled water

Steam peas for 10 minutes. Meanwhile, lay out tomatoes and watercress separately on table.

Prepare sauce: blend tahini and lemon juice. Stir in garlic powder. Slowly add 1/2 c. distilled water, a little at a time, mixing thoroughly after each addition. Continue stirring until sauce is smooth and creamy.

To make burritos place 1 sheet nori flat out on a dry surface. Working quickly, place 1/6 of peas at one lengthwise end. Top with 1/6 of tomatoes, 1/6 sauce, and a handful of watercress. Roll up burrito immediately; place seam side down on a serving platter. Repeat process with remaining nori, sauce, and vegetables. Drizzle ends of each burrito with additional water to moisten. Let burritos sit for 5 minutes.

Serves 1

Calories:

tahini - 380
380 total

*Pressed seaweed sheets found in oriental or health food stores.

**Ground sesame seeds available in health food stores.

Kelp Burritos II

3-4 c. fresh or frozen peas

2 c. bean sprouts

2 tomatoes, chopped

1 bunch watercress or 6 lettuce leaves, chopped

6 sheets nori seaweed*

water (to soften nori)

Tomato Tahini Sauce

1 lg. lemon, juiced

3 T. raw tahini**

3 tomatoes, quartered

3 dashes cayenne pepper

1/2 t. garlic powder

Steam peas until tender, (about 8-10 minutes). Meanwhile, lay out vegetables in groups (ready to stuff nori).

Prepare sauce: blend all sauce ingredients until thick and creamy.

To make burritos, place 1 sheet of nori at a time flat out on a dry surface. Working quickly, place 1/6 of peas at one lengthwise end of nori. Top peas with 1/6 bean sprouts, 1/6 tomatoes, a handful of watercress, and 1/6 sauce. Roll up immediately; place burrito on a long platter. Repeat process with remaining nori sheets and vegetables. If necessary, drizzle ends of burritos with water to moisten. Let kelp burritos sit for 5 minutes.

Serves 1

Calories:
tahini - 285

285 total

Variations:

~Cook 1/2 c. rice or pearl barley with water until tender. Add grain to burrito with vegetables. (Be sure to count additional grain calories.)

~For a slightly sweet sushi taste, make a layer of freshly grated carrots or beets in burritos.

*Pressed seaweed found in oriental or health food stores.

**Ground sesame seeds found in health food stores.

Lettuce Flower Salad

2 hard-boiled eggs

1 sm. onion, chopped

2 c. fresh peas or frozen peas, thawed

1 T. olive oil

20 raw almonds

3 T. fresh parsley, chopped or 1 T. dried parsley

1/2 t. salt (optional)

3 carrots, finely shredded

1 head butter lettuce

tomato wedges and/or daikon radish, (well-scrubbed and sliced)

Grind or finely process eggs, onion, peas, oil, almonds, parsley, and salt. Stir in carrots.

Remove core from lettuce. Place lettuce on a pretty dish, opening up leaves to form a bowl. Mound ground vegetables inside leaves. Garnish with tomato wedges and daikon radish, if desired.

Serves 1

Calories:
eggs - 160
oil - 120
almonds - 120
400 total

Variations:

~Use salad mixture to stuff fresh raw mushrooms or hollowed tomato cups instead of fresh lettuce.

Light and Lovely Salad

Salad Base Ingredients

romaine lettuce, torn up

bronze lettuce, torn up

alfalfa sprouts

bean sprouts

sunflower sprouts (if available)

cherry tomatoes, halved or reg. tomatoes, cut in wedges

jicama, peeled and cut in cubes

carrot, grated

7 oz. baked, pressed tofu, cut in chunks*

Basic Dressing

1-2 lemons, juiced

2 T. olive oil

sprinkles of dry vegetable broth, seasoning, or salt

Salad Additions

arugula or radicchio (for color and flavor)

fresh beets, well-scrubbed, unpeeled, and grated

artichoke hearts (in water)

fresh Chinese pea pods

sunflower seeds...any other fresh vegetable of your choice

Dressing Additions

herbs: marjoram, oregano, thyme, etc.

dry mustard

garlic

fresh dill or dill seeds

caraway seeds

spirulina powder**

Put base ingredients in a large salad bowl. Top with creative salad additions. Dress with basic dressing and any tasty dressing additions. Have fun experimenting. Toss salad well. Let it sit for 5-10 minutes for flavors to blend.

Serves 1

Calories:
baked tofu - 386
oil - 140
626 total

(Note: be sure to count calories of any additions that are not "free and easy" foods.)

*Found in health food stores.

**Nutritive algae available at health food stores.

Luscious Limas With Wild Rice

1 3/4 c. distilled water

1/2 c. raw wild rice

1 pkg. frozen lima beans

2 lg. carrots, sliced

2 stalks broccoli, cut into flowerettes

2 tomatoes, cut in wedges

salt or tamari (optional)

black pepper

garlic powder

In a medium-sized saucepan bring water to a boil. Add rice, cover, lower heat and simmer for 40 minutes, or until rice is tender and water is absorbed.

Meanwhile, steam limas, carrots, and broccoli for 15 minutes. Add tomatoes and steam for 5 more minutes.

To serve, make a bed of wild rice; top rice with vegetables. Season vegetables with salt or tamari, pepper, and garlic powder to taste.

Serves 1

Calories:
wild rice - 280
limas - 283
563 total

Millet Balls in Sweet Tomato Sauce

Millet Balls

1/2 c. raw millet

 1 1/2 c. distilled water

2 T. raw sunflower butter*

1/4 t. black pepper

1/4 t. salt (optional)

1/2 t. garlic powder

2 1/2 T. whole wheat flour

non-stick vegetable spray

Tomato Sauce

1 16 0z. can whole tomatoes

1 6 oz. can tomato paste

2-3 green onions, chopped

1 T. honey

1/2 t. garlic powder

1/4 t. basil

1/8 t. Thyme

Preheat oven to 475 degrees.

Put millet and water in medium saucepan. Bring to a boil. Lower heat, cover and simmer for 15 minutes, or until water is absorbed. Mix in sunflower butter, pepper, salt, and 1/2 t. garlic powder. Roll mixture into 10 or 12 balls. Put flour in a small bowl. Roll each ball in flour until coated with flour. Spray a baking sheet with non-stick spray. Place millet balls on baking sheet. Bake for 30 minutes or until crispy and browned.

While millet balls bake, make sauce. In a medium saucepan, mix all sauce ingredients, breaking up tomatoes.

Simmer, uncovered, until thick; stir occasionally. (Sauce should be ready approximately when millet balls are done.)

To serve, put millet balls in a lovely serving dish. Top balls with sweet tomato sauce or serve sauce on the side as a dip.

Serves 1

Calories:
millet - 310
sunflower butter - 180
flour - 63
honey - 64
617 total

Serving Suggestions:

~Serve millet balls and sauce on top of cooked and drained spaghetti squash for the vegetarian and healthy version of spaghetti and meatballs.

~Accompany millet balls with a fresh green salad.

*Ground sunflower seeds available in health food stores.

Mushrooms Paprika

non-stick vegetable spray

1 T. olive oil

1 lg. onion, chopped

1 green bell pepper, chopped

2 med. tomatoes, chopped

3/4 t. garlic powder

1 c. prepared vegetable broth

1 1/2 T. paprika

1 t. salt (optional)

1/8 t. black pepper

1 lb. mushrooms, cut into chunks

5 dried shitake (oriental mushrooms, soaked for 30 minutes in warm water, sliced (optional)

1 egg

Spray a large frying pan with non-stick spray. Begin to heat then add oil. Sauté onion, green pepper, and tomatoes with garlic powder until onion is tender. Transfer sautéed vegetables to a blender; add broth, and puree until smooth. Return mixture to frying pan and stir in remaining ingredients except the egg. Bring to a boil then lower heat and simmer, uncovered, until liquid is absorbed, (about 15-20 minutes.) Add egg and continue cooking, stirring constantly, until mix is thick and creamy.

Serves 1

Calories:
oil - 120
egg - 80
200 total

Serving Suggestions:

~Accompany mushrooms paprika with a steamy baked potato. (Be sure to count potato calories.)

~Serve this tasty dish with a handful of sprouts, (such as alfalfa or clover) on the sides or around the edges as a garnish. (Note: do not serve Mushrooms Paprika on top of sprouts or it will get watery.)

Pasta with Sweet and Spicy Onions

8 dried shitake mushrooms, soaked for 30 minutes in warm water and sliced

6 large sunchokes (Jerusalem artichokes), scrubbed and thinly sliced

2 lbs. (about 3 lg.) red onions, halved and sliced

5 medium tomatoes, cut in wedges

3/4 t. salt

1 t. garlic powder

1/2 t. basil

1/2 t. rosemary

1 T. (heaping) fresh parsley chopped

dash marjoram

1 lg. bay leaf

1/4 t. black pepper

dash cinnamon

2 t. red wine vinegar

1 c. tomato juice

1 T. honey

1 c. prepared vegetable broth

1/2 c. dried currants

water (for cooking pasta)

4 oz. pasta (fettuccine, egg twists, or any favorite

Combine all ingredients except water and pasta in a large frying pan. Bring to a boil then lower heat, cover and simmer for 20 minutes, stirring occasionally. Uncover and continue simmering, stirring frequently for 10 more minutes, or until vegetables are tender and liquid is reduced and thickened.

Meanwhile, in a large saucepan, bring water to a rapid boil. Cook pasta 7-12 minutes, depending on the type of pasta and your preference in texture. Drain well.

Stir pasta into sweet and spicy onions; serve.

Serves 2

Calories per serving:
honey - 32
currants - 113
pasta - 210
355 total

Pineapple Curry Salad

1/2 lb. mushrooms, sliced

2 green onions, chopped

2 stalks celery, chopped

1 c. pineapple, (fresh or canned) cut in chunks

crisp lettuce or watercress

Pineapple Curry Sauce

1/4 c. pineapple juice

1/2 pkg. (7 oz.) tofu

1 T. raw tahini*

1 T. honey

1 lemon, juiced

1 t. curry powder

1/2 t. salt (optional)

1/8 t. black pepper

Put mushrooms, onions, celery, and pineapple in a mixing bowl. Blend all curry sauce ingredients until smooth and creamy. Pour sauce over vegetables and mix well.

Place lettuce or watercress on a large plate. Mound pineapple curry salad in the center. Garnish with pimiento or fresh parsley, if desired.

Serves 1

Calories:
pineapple - 140
pineapple juice - 35
tofu - 170
tahini - 95
honey - 64
504 total

Variations:

~Add in or top salad with hard-boiled eggs. (Be sure to count egg calories.)

*Ground sesame seeds found in health food stores.

Pineapple Vegetables en Brochette

1 1/2 cans (30 oz.) pineapple chunks (unsweetened), drained (reserve juice)

2 lg. green bell peppers, cut in lg. squares

2 lg. onions, quartered, with layers separated

1 eggplant (1 1/4 lbs.) cut in 1" cubes

3/4 lb. sm. mushrooms

1 1/2 pts. cherry tomatoes

12 oz. tomato paste

4 T. honey

2 T. cider vinegar

1 T. tamari

dash cinnamon

dash dry mustard

Preheat broiler.

In a medium-large saucepan bring reserved pineapple juice to a boil. Reduce heat and add green pepper, onion, and eggplant. Cover and simmer about 5 minutes, or until green pepper is tender-crisp. Remove vegetables with a slotted spoon, (save juice).

Thread green peppers, onions, and eggplant alternately with mushrooms, tomatoes, and pineapple on approximately 16 skewers. Place skewers in a single layer in a large, shallow baking pan. (Use 2 pans if necessary.)

To reserved pineapple juice add tomato paste, honey, vinegar, tamari, cinnamon, and mustard. Bring to a boil, stirring, until sauce is smooth. With a spoon or pastry brush baste skewers with half of the sauce. Broil brochettes a few inches from heat for 5-8 minutes or until crisp. Turn skewers over, baste with remaining sauce, then broil until crisp. (Note: if 2 pans are necessary to accommodate brochettes, broil one pan at a time while keeping the other warm on a lower oven rack.)

To serve, place brochettes on plates and dribble with any remaining pan sauce.

Serves 2

Calories per serving:
pineapple - 140
honey - 128
268 total

Serving Suggestions:

~Serve brochettes on a bed of brown rice or pasta. (Be sure to count rice or pasta calories.)

Ratatouille

non-stick vegetable spray
2 T. olive oil
1 onion, chopped
1 t. garlic powder
1 eggplant, cut in cubes
1 green bell pepper, cut in cubes
1 yellow crookneck squash or zucchini, sliced
1 carrot, sliced
2 T. fresh parsley, chopped or 1 T. dried parsley
2 sunchokes (Jerusalem artichokes) thinly sliced
1 16 oz. can tomatoes, undrained
1 6 oz. can tomato paste
1 t. basil
1 T. honey
1/2 t. salt (optional)
1/4 t. black pepper
1/4 c. distilled water

Spray a large frying pan with non-stick spray. Begin to heat pan then add oil. Sauté onion with garlic powder until browned, (about 5 minutes). Add rest of ingredients, except water. Stir well, cover, and simmer for 8 minutes. Add water to pan, stir well then cover and simmer for 15 more minutes, or until vegetables are tender. (Add more water, if necessary.)

Serves 1

Calories:
oil - 240
honey - 64

304 total

Serving Suggestions:

~Use the ratatouille as an interesting vegetable stuffing. For example, instead of cutting up the entire eggplant, scoop out the pulp and use it in the ratatouille recipe above. Meanwhile, steam the eggplant shells until tender. Stuff the shells with the ratatouille when done.

~Or, steam, a seeded red or green bell pepper shell until tender. (Onions or different squashes can be versatile containers for the ratatouille, too.) Stuff with ratatouille.

Santa Barbara Gourmet Salad
With Maple Poppy Seed Vinaigrette

Salad

1 sm. head butter lettuce

1/2 cucumber, peeled and thinly sliced

1/4 lb. mushrooms, thinly sliced

cherry tomatoes, halved

jicama, peeled and cut in thin sticks

fresh Chinese pea pods

1 can hearts of palm, drained and halved lengthwise

1 can artichoke hearts (in water), drained

other exotic vegetables (e.g. red bell pepper, arugula, watercress, etc)

Vinaigrette

2 T. red wine vinegar

1 t. Dijon mustard

1/3 t. salt (optional)

2 T. olive oil

1 T. pure maple syrup

1 T. distilled water

1 t. tamari

1/2 t. tarragon

1 t. poppy seeds

2 T. fresh parsley, finely chopped

On a large beautiful platter make a bed of butter lettuce leaves. Decoratively arrange all other salad vegetables on leaves.

Make vinaigrette: in a small bowl, mix vinegar, mustard, and salt. Slowly whisk in oil. Blend in rest of ingredients.

To serve, drizzle maple poppy seed vinaigrette over salad.

Serves 1

Calories:
oil - 240
maple syrup - 50
poppy seed   - 13
303 total

Serving Suggestions:

~Top salad with slices of hard-boiled eggs. (Be sure to count egg calories.)

Saucey Lentil Enchiladas

1 c. tomato juice

2 lg. onions, chopped

1 1/2 t. garlic powder

3 lg. or 6 sm. tomatoes, chopped

2 lg. carrots, grated

1 T. curry powder

2 T. fresh cilantro, chopped

1 T. lemon juice

1 t. cumin

1/4 t. cayenne pepper

2 dashes ginger

2 t. salt (optional)

1/4 t. black pepper

1 c. lentils

2 bunches fresh spinach, stems removed

2 c. liquid vegetable broth

12 sheets nori seaweed*

30 black olives, sliced

Sauce

non-stick vegetable spray

4 green onions, chopped

15-16 oz. tomato sauce

4 tomatoes, chopped

1 fresh green chile (about 2 oz.), chopped or 2 canned chiles, drained and chopped

1/8 t. cayenne pepper

1/2 t. oregano

1/2 t. basil

In a large saucepan, combine tomato juice, onions, and garlic. Cook over medium heat, uncovered, until onion is tender. Add tomatoes, carrots, curry, cilantro, lemon juice, cumin, cayenne, ginger, salt, and pepper. Continue cooking over medium heat, stirring occasionally, until tomatoes are tender, (about 8-10 minutes). Stir in lentils, spinach, and broth. Bring to a boil, cover, then lower heat and simmer for 30 minutes. Uncover, bring to a boil and cook for about 20 more minutes, stirring frequently, until liquid is absorbed.

While vegetables are simmering, make sauce. Spray a medium-sized saucepan with non-stick spray. Sauté green onions until soft, about 3-5 minutes. Add remaining sauce ingredients. Simmer, uncovered, for 30 minutes, or until thickened.

To assemble enchiladas, put nori sheets -2 at a time- on a dry surface. Put 2 heaping tablespoons of lentil mix at lengthwise end of each nori sheet. Roll up quickly; set on a serving platter, seam side down. Repeat process with all nori sheets using up the lentil mixture. Pour sauce over enchiladas and sprinkle with olives.

Serves 2

Calories per serving:
lentils - 323
olives - 75
398 total

*Found in oriental or health food stores

Savory Baked Eggplant

non-stick vegetable spray

1 very lg. eggplant or 6 med. Japanese eggplants, cut in cubes

3 lg. tomatoes, cut in chunks

1/2 c. vegetarian baco bits

1 sm. onion, chopped

3/4 t. garlic powder

1/4 t. black pepper

3/4 t. rosemary

3 dashes cayenne pepper

1/4 c. red wine vinegar

2 T. olive oil

Preheat oven to 450 degrees.

Spray a medium-large baking pan (approximately 12" x 9"x 2") with non-stick spray. Spread eggplant cubes in pan. Top eggplant with remaining ingredients. Bake for 45 minutes, stirring occasionally, or until eggplant is very soft and flavors are well-blended. Serve hot or cold.

Serves 1

Calories:
baco bits - 192
oil - 240
432 total

Sea Stew

1/3 pkg. hiziki or arame seaweed*
1/3 pkg. dulse seaweed*
1 c. fresh or frozen corn
7 mushrooms, halved
3 oz. fresh or frozen Chinese pea pods
1/3 lb. fresh bean sprouts
dash cayenne pepper
dash dry mustard
1 T. honey
1 T. spirulina algae**
1 c. distilled water
1 1/2 cubes or 1 1/2 t. vegetable bouillon
1/2 pkg. (7 oz.) tofu, cut in cubes

Rinse hiziki and dulse under cold water to remove any sand.

In a large saucepan, combine all ingredients, except tofu. Bring stew to a boil. Cover pan, lower heat and simmer until seaweeds and vegetables are semi-soft, (about 20 minutes). Stir in tofu.

Serves 1

Calories:
corn - 148
honey - 64
algae - 80
tofu - 170
462 total

*Hiziki and dulse are available in oriental or health food stores.

**A powdered, flavorful algae found in health food stores.

Sesame Eggplant Bake

2 bunches fresh spinach, chopped

non-stick vegetable spray

2 lg. or 3 sm. eggplants

2 T. olive oil

2 lg. onions, chopped

1 lg. green bell pepper, chopped

1 1/2 t. garlic powder

3 lg. tomatoes, cut in wedges

3 scallions, chopped

1 bunch watercress, with stems removed, chopped

2 T. lemon juice

1 1/2 t. oregano

1 t. salt (optional)

1/4 t. black pepper

1/4 c. sesame seeds

Preheat broiler.

Steam spinach for 5 minutes or until tender; set aside.

Spray a baking sheet with non-stick spray. Slice eggplants lengthwise, 1/3 inch thick. Then cut each slice into 3 lengthwise strips. Arrange eggplant on baking sheet in a single layer. Broil 7-10 minutes or until browned. Turn eggplant slices over, broil until browned. Put aside; set oven to bake, 400 degrees.

Spray a large frying pan with non-stick spray. Begin to heat then add oil. Sauté onions and green pepper with garlic until crisp-tender (about 7 minutes). Add tomatoes, spinach, scallions, and watercress. Simmer, uncovered, 10 minutes, stirring occasionally. Add lemon juice, oregano, salt, and pepper.

Meanwhile, spread sesame seeds on a small baking sheet. Bake a few minutes until browned.

In a 2 1/2 quart covered casserole put a few tablespoons of the vegetable sauce. Top with 1/3 of eggplant slices. Cover eggplant with 1/3 remaining sauce, repeating layers, ending with sauce. Cover casserole and bake for 10 minutes.

Sprinkle eggplant with sesame seeds and serve.

Serves 2

Calories per serving:
oil - 120
sesame seeds - 94
214 total

Spaghetti Squash Bowl of Mandarin Vegetables

non-stick vegetable spray

1 spaghetti squash (about 8"long), sliced in half lengthwise and seeded 1 sm. onion, chopped

1 sm. green bell pepper, sliced

1 red bell pepper, sliced

1 lg. stalk celery, thinly sliced

1 1/4 lbs. mushrooms, quartered

1 T. orange rind, grated

1/2 t. fresh ginger root, peeled and grated

3 T. honey

1 T. cider vinegar

1/2 c. orange juice

1/2 c. liquid vegetable broth

1 T. tamari

1 T. arrowroot, mixed with 1 T. water to a "paste"*

1 orange, peeled and cut in chunks

2 T. raw sunflower seeds

Preheat oven to 400 degrees.

Spray a baking sheet with non-stick spray. Put squash halves, cut side down, on sheet and bake for 30 minutes, or until tender when pierced. Remove from oven and set aside.

While squash bakes, combine onion, green pepper, red pepper, celery, and mushrooms in a medium-sized baking pan. In a medium-sized saucepan, combine orange rind, ginger, honey, vinegar, orange juice, broth, and tamari. Simmer, uncovered, 5 minutes. Add arrowroot paste, stirring, until mixture thickens. Stir in orange chunks. Pour sauce over vegetables in baking pan. Bake, uncovered, for 25 minutes.

Scoop "spaghetti" out of squash halves, being careful not to break shells. Mix "spaghetti" with mandarin vegetables, then mound into squash shells. Sprinkle with sunflower seeds.

Serves 1

Calories:
honey - 192
orange juice - 60
arrowroot - 29
orange - 80
sunflower seeds - <u>102</u>
463 total

*A natural substitute for cornstarch found in health food stores.

Spinach Dumplings Marinara

Marinara

8 oz. tomato sauce

6 oz. tomato paste

3 med. tomatoes, chopped

2 green onions, chopped

1/4 c. distilled water

2 t. honey

1/8 t. salt (optional)

1/2 t. rosemary

1/2 t. garlic powder

1/2 t. oregano

1/2 t. basil

1/4 t. thyme

Dumplings

2 eggs, separated

pinch cream of tartar

1/4 t. salt (optional)

1/2 c. matzoh meal

1/8 t. black pepper

1 pkg. frozen chopped spinach, thawed and well-drained

water

sprigs of fresh parsley(optional)

Put all marinara ingredients in a medium saucepan. Simmer, uncovered, over medium-low heat one-half hour or until thickened.

Meanwhile, make dumplings: beat egg whites with cream of tartar until stiff, but not dry. In a separate bowl, beat egg yolks with 1/8 t. salt. Fold whites into yolks. Slowly add matzoh meal to egg mixture with remaining salt and pepper. Stir in spinach. Form mixture into 10-12 small balls (dumplings). Fill a large saucepan 3/4 full with water. Bring water to a rapid boil. Drop dumplings, one by one, into water, making sure to keep water boiling. Boil dumplings, uncovered, 15 minutes.

To serve, place dumplings in a serving dish. Top with marinara sauce. Garnish with fresh parsley sprigs, if desired.

Serves 1

Calories:
honey - 22
eggs - 160
matzoh meal - <u>220</u>
402 total

Serving Suggestions:

~Serve spinach dumplings marinara on top of cooked and drained spaghetti squash.

~Clean and pat dry a bunch of fresh spinach. Make a bed of spinach leaves in a serving bowl and top with dumplings and marinara.

Spinach Noodle Ring With Tomatoes Creole

Noodle Ring

2 oz. bean threads*

warm water

1 bunch fresh spinach or 1 pkg. frozen spinach, chopped

3 green onions, chopped

2 eggs, separated

1 1/2 t. olive oil

1/4 t. paprika

1/4 t. salt (optional)

3 1/2 oz. (28 lg.) ripe black olives, pitted and sliced

non-stick vegetable spray

Tomatoes Creole

4 med. tomatoes, chopped

1 med. green bell pepper, chopped

1 lg. onion, chopped

1/4 c. distilled water

3/4 t. salt (optional)

1/4 t. paprika

3/4 t. curry powder

1 T. honey

1 1/2 T. whole wheat flour

Preheat oven to 375 degrees.

Soak bean threads in warm water for 20 minutes; drain well.

Steam spinach and green onions for 10 minutes until tender. Beat 2 egg yolks, oil, paprika, and salt. Stir in bean threads, steamed vegetables, and olives, breaking apart bean threads. Beat remaining 2 egg whites until frothy; fold into vegetable/bean thread mixture. Spray a ring mold with non-stick spray; pour mixture. Place mold in a pan filled with hot water. Bake 30-40 minutes or until ring holds its shape.

Meanwhile, make tomatoes creole. Put tomatoes, green pepper, onion, and water in a medium sauce pan. Bring to a boil then lower heat and simmer, uncovered, 10 minutes; stir occasionally. Add salt paprika, curry and honey. Simmer, uncovered, 10 or more minutes. Stir in flour, slowly, mixing until creole is thick.

To serve, loosen edges of mold with a knife. Invert onto a large plate. Fill center of spinach noodle ring with tomatoes creole.

Serves 1

Calories:
bean threads - 194
eggs - 160
oil - 60
olives - 140
honey - 64
flour - 38
656 total

Variations:

~Instead of filling noodle ring with tomatoes creole, fill with one-half recipe of ratatouille.

*Thin, clear noodle threads available at oriental food stores.

Stuffed Cauliflower With Tahini Tarragon Sauce

Stuffed Cauliflower

1 lg. cauliflower, leaves removed

6 mushrooms, sliced

1 med. onion, chopped

3 1/2 oz. baked, pressed tofu, cut in small cubes*

1/4 c. pimiento, sliced or 1/2 tomato chopped

1/4 t. garlic powder

1 T. fresh parsley, chopped

3 dashes black pepper

1/4 c. distilled water

Tahini Tarragon Sauce

non-stick vegetable spray

1 onion, chopped

2 green onions, chopped

1 lg. carrot, grated

1 c. plus 2 T. distilled water

1 T. miso**

1 1/2 t. honey

1 T. raw tahini***

2 T. whole wheat flour

1 bunch watercress, chopped or 4 leaves lettuce, sliced

1 T. fresh parsley, chopped

1/2 t. tarragon

Preheat oven to 350 degrees.

Place steamer rack in large saucepan. Place cauliflower on one-half of steamer; put mushrooms and onions on other half. Steam vegetables for 10 to 15 minutes or until cauli-flower is crisp-tender.

Place cauliflower in a 1 1/2 quart casserole. Cut out center flowerettes (reserve), to create a hollow, pushing outer flowerettes to edges of casserole. Chop reserved flowerettes; mix with mushrooms, onion and remaining ingredients except water. Stuff into cauliflower hollow. Pour water around edges of cauliflower. Bake uncovered for 20 minutes.

Meanwhile, prepare sauce: spray a medium saucepan with non-stick spray. Saute onions and carrot until slightly browned. Mix 2 T water, miso, honey, and tahini until smooth. Stir into vegetables. Slowly add flour. Mixing until blended. Add remaining 1 cup water; blend well. Mix on watercress, parsley, and tarragon. Simmer 5 minutes, stirring constantly.

To serve, place cauliflower on a serving dish and smother with sauce.

Serves 1

Calories:
tofu - 194
miso - 35
honey - 32
tahini - 95
flour - 50
406 total

*Available in health food stores.

**Soybean paste available in oriental or health food stores.

***Ground sesame seeds available in health food stores.

Stuffed Grape Leaves With Honey Lemon Sauce

4 stalks celery, chopped

1 bunch red chard, chopped with 2" of stems

3 lg. carrots grated

1 c. cooked garbanzo beans (chick peas), drained and mashed

1 T. capers

1 t. cumin

1 t. tarragon

1 t. dill weed or seed

20 (approx.) grape leaves, rinsed; (one jar should be enough)

Honey Lemon Sauce

1 whole egg

1 egg yolk

1 lemon, juiced

1 T. honey

1/2 t. salt (optional)

1 c. distilled water

1 T. arrowroot, mixed with a little water to make a paste*

Steam celery, chard, and carrots until tender, (about 15 minutes). Mix with garbanzos, capers, cumin, tarragon and dill.

Lay out grape leaves, a few at a time. Put a large spoonful of vegetable mix (about 2 T.) on stem of each leaf. Fold sides of leaves over filling; roll up leaves. Place stuffed leaves on serving dish, seam side down. Repeat process until stuffing is used up.

Make sauce: beat whole egg and yolk. Slowly beat in lemon juice, honey, and salt. Bring water to a boil in a small sauce pam. Stir in arrowroot paste and boil for 1 minute. Stir hot mixture into egg mix very slowly. Return sauce to pan and cook over low heat, uncovered, stirring until thick. Pour sauce over grape leaves. Sprinkle with fresh dill, if desired.

Serves 1

Calories:
garbanzos - 338
whole egg   - 80
egg yolk - 80
honey - 64
arrowroot   - 29
591 total

Variations:

~For a warm dish, heat grape leaves in a moderate oven, (about 350 degrees for one-half hour then top with sauce.

~Steamed chard leaves may be used instead of grape leaves.

*A natural substitute for cornstarch found in health food stores.

Stuffed Green Peppers and Onion Cream With Olive Sauce

2 lg. onions, whole

1/2 c. raw wild rice

1/2 lb. mushrooms, sliced

2 c. distilled water

1/4 t. garlic powder

3 lg. green bell peppers

water (for boiling)

3 sm. tomatoes, chopped

2 T. pimiento, chopped

1 T. capers

1/2 t. salt (optional)

1/8 t. black pepper

1/4 c. liquid vegetable broth

Olive Sauce

1 T. olive oil

1 sm. onion, chopped

2 T. whole wheat flour

1 c. liquid vegetable broth

2 oz. (approx. 20) green olives, stuffed and sliced

Put 2 whole onions directly on oven rack. Bake 375 degrees for 70-90 minutes or until tender.

Meanwhile, put rice, mushrooms, 2 c. water and garlic powder in a medium saucepan. Cover and bring to boil then lower heat and simmer for 45 minutes or until rice is tender.

While rice cooks, slice stems off bell peppers (to form "hats.") Remove inner seeds and membranes. Bring water to a boil in a large saucepan. Plunge peppers and caps into water, cover pan, simmer 5-8 minutes, or until peppers are tender-crisp. Drain well.

Combine rice mixture tomatoes, pimiento, capers, salt and pepper. Stuff mixture into bell peppers: replace caps. Arrange peppers in baking dish. Pour 1/4 c. broth around peppers; bake 15 minutes (at 375 degrees with whole onions.

Make sauce: heat oil in a small sauce pan. Add chopped onion and sauté until golden. Mix in flour. Add 1 c. broth slowly, stirring well until sauce is creamy, and olives. Simmer for 5 more minutes.

To serve, smother stuffed green peppers with olive sauce. Cut roots ends off baked onions. Squeeze out inner cream to serve as a flavorful condiment with peppers; season with salt, pepper and paprika, if desired.

Serves 1

Calories:
wild rice - 280
oil - 120
flour - 50
olives - 74
524 total

Stuffed Tomatoes With Vegetarian Chopped "Liver"

1 lb. fresh string beans, stems removed

1 stalk celery, chopped

1/2 lb. mushrooms, sliced

2 med. onions, chopped

2 eggs, hard-boiled

1/4 c. fresh parsley, chopped

1/4 c. raw walnuts, chopped

1 T. olive oil

1 T. garlic powder

1/2 t. thyme

1/8-1/4 t. black pepper

dash nutmeg

salt to taste (optional)

6 very lg. tomatoes

sprigs of fresh parsley

Steam string beans, celery, mushrooms, and onions for 10 minutes, or until tender. Grind thoroughly in a grinder, food processor, or blender with eggs, chopped parsley, and walnuts. Mix in rest of ingredients, except tomatoes and parsley sprigs, to make chopped "liver."

Cut a small "hat" off tomatoes. Scoop out tomato cup pulp. Fill tomatoes with chopped "liver." Replace tomato tops, if desired. Garnish with parsley sprigs.

Serves 1

Calories:
eggs - 160

walnuts - 200
oil - <u>120</u>
480 total

Variations:

~Instead of stuffing large tomatoes, fill mushrooms or let-tuce cups with this delicious vegetable mixture.

Succulent Okra

non-stick vegetable spray

1 T. olive oil

1 lg. onion, sliced

1/2 t. garlic powder

6 oz. tomato paste

4 med. tomatoes, diced

1 c. V-8 or tomato juice

1/4 c. lemon juice

1 t. honey

1/2 t. salt (optional)

1/4 t. black pepper

1 lb. fresh sm. okra

3 oz. (about 35) ripe green olives with pimientos, sliced

Spray a large frying pan with non-stick spray. Begin to heat, then add oil. Sauté onion and garlic until lightly browned. Stir in tomato paste, tomatoes, V-8, lemon juice, honey, salt, and pepper. Bring to a boil, lower heat, cover, and simmer 15 minutes.

Add okra and olives to tomato mixture. Stir well. Cover and simmer for 30 more minutes, stirring occasionally.

Serves 1

Calories:
oil - 120
honey - 22
olives - 125
267 total

Serving Suggestion:

~Serve with a crisp, baked potato. (Be sure to count potato calories.)

Sumptuous Apples and Onions in a Sunchoke Nest

7 1/2 oz. tofu, cut in 1/2" cubes

1 green apple, chopped

3 lg. stalks celery, diced (including leaves)

1 c. distilled water

non-stick vegetable spray

1 T. olive oil

1 lg. onion, chopped

1 t. garlic powder

1 1/2 t. ginger

1/2 lb. mushrooms, sliced

2 t. curry powder.

2 T. whole wheat flour

2 T. miso*

1 T. honey

3 T. ketchup (a brand made with honey, if possible)

1 lb. sunchokes (Jerusalem artichokes), scrubbed and grated

Combine first four ingredients in a medium-sized saucepan. Bring to a boil, then cover and lower heat to simmer.

Meanwhile, spray a medium-sized frying pan with non-stick spray. Begin to heat; then add oil. Sauté onion until brown and tender. Stir in garlic and ginger. Add mushrooms. Sauté mushrooms until tender. Mix in curry and flour, stirring constantly for 1 minute. Remove pan from heat.

In a small bowl cream miso with 1/3 cup broth from apple and celery saucepan. Stir miso mix into onion and mushroom mix in frying pan. Add honey and ketchup; stir to form a thick, smooth sauce. Set aside for a minute.

Steam grated artichokes for 10 minutes. Meanwhile, pour sauce into apple saucepan, cover and simmer for 10 minutes, stirring constantly.

To serve, press grated artichoke gently against sides of two shallow serving bowls to forms "nests". Fill nests with apple mix.

Serves 1 or 2

Calories:
tofu - 170
apple - 80
oil - 120
flour - 50
miso - 70
honey - 64
ketchup - 48
602 (if recipe serves 1)
301 (if recipe serves 2)

Serving Suggestions:

~Try topping this sumptuous dish with any of these: sliced bananas, shredded coconut, raisins, diced green apple, peanuts, almonds, and/or hard-boiled eggs. (Be sure to count calories of these additional items.)

*Soybean paste found in oriental or health food stores.

Sweet and Sour Baco Beans

1 1/2 lb. fresh green beans, trimmed and halved

1 lb. mushrooms, halved

non-stick vegetable spray

1 onion, thinly sliced

1/2 c. cider vinegar

2 T. honey

1/4 c. pimientos

1/2 c. vegetarian baco bits

In a large saucepan, steam green beans and mushrooms for 15 minutes or until beans are tender-crisp. Drain well; set aside.

Removed steamer rack from saucepan. Spray with non-stick spray. Sauté onion for a few minutes until slightly browned. Add vinegar and honey. Stir over medium-low heat for 5 minutes or until onion is tender. Add green beans and mushrooms, pimiento and baco bits. Mix well until all flavors are blended.

Serves 1

Calories:
honey - 128
baco bits - <u>192</u>
320 total

Sweet Red Curry

3/4 c. distilled water

1/4 c. raw wild rice

non-stick vegetable spray

1 T. olive oil

2 onions, chopped

1 stalk celery, chopped

1 red bell pepper, sliced

2 tomatoes, finely chopped

1 tart green apple, cored and diced

1 c. fresh or frozen peas

1/4 c. dried, unsweetened coconut, shredded

1 T. honey

1 t. curry powder mixed with 2 T. distilled water

1 t. cardamom or coriander

1 T. tomato paste

In a medium-sized saucepan bring water to a boil. Add rice, cover and simmer for 40 minutes, or until rice is tender and water is absorbed. (Add more water if necessary.)

Meanwhile, spray a large frying pan with non-stick spray. Begin to heat pan, then add oil. Sauté onions, celery, and bell pepper until tender-crisp, (about 8-10 minutes). Add remaining ingredients. Cook, uncovered, over medium heat until apple pieces are tender, (about 12-15 minutes).

Serve sweet red curry over wild rice.

Serves 1

Calories:
wild rice - 105

oil - 120
apple - 90
coconut - 156
honey - 64
535 total

Tangy Hummus Salad

1 15 oz. can garbanzo beans (chick peas), drained and mashed

2 T. raw tahini*

1 1/2 sm. lemons, juiced

garlic powder (to taste)

4 oz. fresh green sprouts, (i.e. alfalfa, clover, sunflower, etc., alone or combined)

3 carrots, finely shredded

1/2 cucumber, peeled, halved lengthwise, and sliced

2 lg. tomatoes, cut in wedges or halved cherry tomatoes

paprika (optional)

sprigs of fresh parsley or dill

To make hummus: mix garbanzos, tahini, lemon juice, and garlic powder.

To assemble: on a large plate, make a bed of sprouts. Mound carrots in center of sprouts, making a well in center of carrots. Alternate slices of tomato and cucumber around and on top of sprouts. Mound hummus in carrot well. Garnish with paprika and/or sprigs of fresh parsley or dill.

Serves 1

Calories:
garbanzos - 507
tahini - 190
697 total

Variations:

~For a little more pizazz add a dash of cayenne pepper or cumin to hummus.

Ground sesame seeds found in health food stores.

Tenderleeks

9 med. leeks

12 oz. tomato juice

1/2 lb. mushrooms, sliced

5 tomatoes, chopped

3 oz. (about 35) ripe green olives with pimiento, sliced

1/4 c. fresh parsley, chopped

1 t. salt (optional)

1/4 t. black pepper

1 t. garlic powder

3/4 t. each: basil, marjoram, oregano, rosemary

2 eggs, beaten

Trim ends and leaves off leeks, leaving about 2 inches of leaves. Cut leeks in half lengthwise, wash well, and discard outer tough leaves. Place leeks and tomato juice in a large frying pan. Bring to a boil, then lower heat, cover, and simmer for 10 minutes. Add remaining ingredients except eggs, stir gently. Simmer, uncovered, for 10 minutes, or until sauce is reduced and leeks are tender. Add eggs, continue simmering, stirring frequently, until mix is thick and creamy.

Serves 1

Calories:
olives - 125
eggs - 160
285 total

Serving Suggestions:

~Decorate tenderleeks with sliced or halved hard-boiled eggs. (Be sure to count egg calories.)

Thick and Rich Noodley Beans

4 1/2 c. distilled water

1/2 c. dry kidney beans

2 bay leaves

2 lg. carrots, sliced

3 lg. celery stalks, sliced (with leaves included)

3/4 t. salt (optional)

4 dashes black pepper

1/2 t. basil

1/2 t. thyme

1 t. sage

1 t. garlic powder

6 oz. tomato paste

1 oz. fettuccine noodles

Put 3 1/2 c. water, beans and bay leaves in a medium saucepan. Cover, bring to a boil, then lower heat and simmer for 1/2 hour. Add carrots, celery, salt pepper, basil, thyme, sage and garlic powder. Bring to a boil again, mix well, cover and simmer for 15 more minutes or until vegetables are tender.

Put 1/3 to 1/2 vegetables in a blender with a little of the soup broth, puree. (A higher vegetable to broth ratio will make mixture thicker.) Pour puree back into saucepan with remaining 1 c. water and tomato paste; stir well. Break noodles into vegetable mix, cover, and simmer for 10-15 more minutes, stirring frequently, until noodles are tender and mixture is thick and chewy. (Add more water, if necessary for noodles to finish cooking or if a thinner noodle beans is preferred.

Serves 1

Calories:
kidney beans - 317
fettuccine - 210
527 total

Serving Suggestions:

~Serve this rib-sticking dish in an earthy, wooden bowl and garnish with fresh parsley or fresh greens.

Variation:

~Instead of fettuccine, use any other favorite pasta or noodle.

Tiger Lily and Tree Ear Spice Soup

5 dried Chinese fungi (tree ears)*

4 dried shitake mushrooms

10 dried tiger lily buds (golden needles)*

warm water

3 c. distilled water

3 cubes or 3 t. vegetable bouillon

1 sm. can (7 oz.) bamboo shoots, drained

1/2 pkg. (7 oz.) tofu, cut in cubes

1 t. tamari

1/4 t. salt (optional)

1/4 t. black pepper

1 t. honey

2 t. cider vinegar

2 t. arrowroot**

3 t. water

1 egg, lightly beaten

1 t. olive oil

Soak tree ears, mushrooms, and tiger lily buds in warm water for 30 minutes. Drain. Slice tree ears and mushrooms.

In a medium-sized saucepan, combine tree ears, mushrooms, tiger lily buds, 3 c. distilled water, bouillon, bamboo, and tofu. Bring to a boil then reduce heat and simmer, uncovered for 10 minutes.

Stir tamari, salt, pepper, honey and vinegar into soup. Mix arrowroot with 3 t. water until pasty. Add a little hot soup to arrowroot paste, blend well, then pour mix back into soup. Bring soup to a boil and cook for 2 minutes stirring frequently. Remove from heat; gently stir in egg and oil until egg becomes stringy.

Serves 1

Calories:
tofu - 170
honey - 22
arrowroot - 19
egg - 80
oil - 40
331 total

*Both fungi and golden needles are found in oriental grocery stores. **Healthy substitute for cornstarch found in health food stores.

Vegetables in Light Ginger Sauce

1 red bell pepper, seeded and thinly sliced

1 green bell pepper, seeded and thinly sliced

1/2 lb. mushrooms, sliced

1 onion, thinly sliced

2 stalks broccoli, cut in flowerettes with 2 inch stems

4 lg. sunchokes (Jerusalem artichokes), scrubbed and thinly sliced or 1 sm. can water chestnuts, thinly sliced

2 carrots, diagonally sliced

1 zucchini, diagonally sliced

8 oz. can bamboo shoots, drained

3 oz. fresh Chinese pea pods, trimmed, or 1/2 pkg. frozen pea pods, thawed

2 T. olive oil

2 T. tamari

1/4 t. ginger powder

2 t. honey

alfalfa sprouts

In a large saucepan, steam all vegetables, except sprouts, until tender-crisp, (about 12-15 minutes). Drain vegetables; place in a large serving bowl.

Mix oil, tamari, and ginger in a small bowl. Pour oil mixture over vegetables, then drizzle with honey. Toss well. Garnish with a ring of alfalfa sprouts, if desired.

Serves 1

Calories:
oil - 240
honey - 43

283 total

Variations:

~Steam fresh pineapple chunks along with vegetables for a tropical touch. (Count pineapple calories.)

~Top vegetables with cashews, almonds, or a favorite nut or seed. (Be sure to count added calories.)

Vegetable Pate

2 carrots
2 stalks celery w/ leaves
1 zucchini
1 green bell pepper, seeded
1/2 lb. mushrooms, chopped
1 leeks or 1 onion, finely chopped
1 c. fresh parsley, chopped
1 egg, beaten
1/4 c. matzoh meal
4 T. raw tahini*
1/4 c. tamari
1 lg. lemon, juiced
1 t. caraway seed
1 t. basil
1 t. dill weed
1/2 t. marjoram
1/2 t. thyme
1/8 t. oregano
1/4 t. dry mustard
1 t. salt (optional)
1/4 t. black pepper
non-stick vegetable spray
4 sheets nori seaweed**
paprika

Preheat oven to 400 degrees.

Grind carrots, celery, zucchini, and green pepper into a large mixing bowl. Add rest of ingredients except vegetable spray, nori, and paprika; mix well.

Spray a loaf pan with non-stick spray. Run nori sheets one by one, quickly under cool water (to make it workable.) Place 2 sheets of nori across bottom and width of loaf pan, overlapping sheets across bottom of pan. Let sheets overhang edges. Fold other 2 sheets of nori to fit in pan lengthwise, again overhanging top edges. Pour in vegetable mix. Pat down to fit pan. Sprinkle loaf with paprika then fold overhanging edges of nori over top of loaf. Bake loaf for 45 minutes. Run a knife around edges and invert loaf onto serving platter. Serve hot or cold.

Serves 1

Calories:
egg - 80
matzoh meal - 110
tahini - 392
582 total

Serving Suggestions:

~Place sliced tomatoes down center of pate. Garnish loaf with sprigs of fresh parsley or edible flowers.

*Ground sesame seeds found in health food stores.

**Pressed seaweed available in oriental or health food stores.

Vegetables Stroganoff

1 onion, cut in wedges

1/2 lb. mushrooms, halved

3 sunchokes (Jerusalem artichokes), sliced

2 carrots, diagonally sliced

1 pt. cherry tomatoes or 2 tomatoes, cut in wedges

water (for cooking pasta)

2 oz. Fettuccine

non-stick vegetable spray

1 onion, chopped

2 scallions, chopped

2 T. distilled water

1 T. raw tahini*

1 T. miso**

1 1/2 t. honey

2 T. whole wheat flour

1 c. distilled water

1/2 head romaine lettuce sliced in strips

1 T. (heaping) fresh parsley, chopped

1/4 t. tarragon

1/4 t. garlic powder

1/8 t. black pepper

1/4 t. salt (optional)

In a large saucepan, steam wedge-cut onion, mushrooms, sunchokes, carrots, and tomatoes until crisp-tender (about 8-10 minutes.) Remove saucepan from heat with cover on; set aside.

Bring water to a rapid boil. Add fettuccine; cook until al dente (about 10-15 minutes).

Meanwhile, make sauce: spray a large frying pan with non-stick spray. Sauté chopped onion and scallions until lightly browned. In a small mixing bowl, blend 2 T. distilled water, tahini, miso, and honey to a paste. Stir into onions over medium-low heat. Add flour and mix well. Combine 1 c. distilled water and half of lettuce; slowly stir into onion mixture and bring to a boil. Add remaining lettuce, parsley, and seasonings. Simmer, uncovered and stirring frequently, about 8-10 minutes, or until thickened.

Drain fettuccine and vegetables. Place fettuccine on a serving plate; top with vegetables and stroganoff sauce. Garnish with additional parsley, if desired.

Serves 1

Calories:
fettuccine - 210
tahini - 95
miso - 35
honey - 32
flour - 50
422 total

Serving Suggestions:

~Garnish with cashews. (Be sure to count calories.)

~Serve on top of a baked potato. (Count calories.)

Variations:

~To reduce calories, omit fettuccine.

*Ground sesame seeds available in health food stores.

**Soybean paste available in oriental or health stores.

Warm and Hearty Bean Bowl

1/4 c. split peas

1/4 c. dry pearl barley

2 c. distilled water

1 sm. onion, chopped

2 stalks celery (with leaves), sliced

2 lg. carrots, sliced

1/2 t. garlic powder

1/2 t. salt (optional)

3 dashes cayenne pepper

1/8 t. black pepper

3/4 t. cumin

1/2 t. curry powder

1 bunch red chard or spinach, stems removed, sliced in strips

6 sheets nori seaweed, cut into bite-size pieces*

In a medium saucepan, combine split peas, barley, and water. Bring to a boil, then lower heat, cover, and simmer for 20 minutes. Add onion, celery, carrots, and seasonings; stir well. Add chard (set it on top of vegetables). (Pan will be stuffed at first, but later ingredients will shrink down.) Bring to a boll again, cover, then simmer for another 20 minutes or until grains are soft and water is absorbed; stir occasionally. (Add more water or tamari, if necessary, to moisten vegetables until finish cooking.) Stir in nori, a few pieces at a time, until softened. Serve and sprinkle with tamari if desired.

Serves 1

Calories:

split peas - 174
pearl barley - <u>175</u>
349 total

*Pressed seaweed available in oriental or health food stores.

Warm Green Beans and Spinach With Tomato Miso Dressing

1 lb. fresh green beans, cut in 2" pieces

2 bunches fresh spinach, stems removed

1 1/2 T. tahini*

1 T. honey

1 1/2 T. miso**

1 T. cider vinegar

1/2 t. garlic powder

3 tomatoes, quartered

8 shitake (oriental) mushrooms, soaked in warm water for 20 minutes or 10

fresh mushrooms steamed for 8 minutes

In a large saucepan, steam green beans for 10 minutes or until tender. Add spinach and steam for 3-5 minutes or until leaves are wilted but not soggy. Drain green beans and spinach in colander, pressing out moisture.

Put tahini, honey, miso, vinegar, garlic, and tomatoes in food processor or blender. Blend until smooth.

To serve, place green beans and spinach in a wooden bowl. Smother with tomato miso dressing. Top with mushrooms.

Serves 1

Calories:
tahini - 143
honey - 64
miso - 53
260 total

*Ground sesame seeds found in health food stores.

**Soybean paste found in oriental or health food stores.

Wild Rice and Raisin Stuffed Eggplant

1/2 c. raw wild rice

2 c. distilled water

1 lg. eggplant, halved lengthwise

non-stick vegetable spray

1 onion, finely chopped

1/2 c. raisins or dried currants

1/3 c. raw almonds, slivered

2 t. cilantro or coriander

salt and pepper to taste

Tomato Curry Sauce

1 t. garlic powder

1 1/2 t. curry powder

5 sm. tomatoes, diced

1 sm. can (6 oz.) tomato paste

1 T. Honey

Preheat oven to 450 degrees.

Put water in a medium-sized saucepan and bring to a boil. Add rice, cover lower heat and simmer for 45 minutes or until rice is tender.

Meanwhile, make 1/2" deep cut around the inside perimeter of the cut sides of the eggplant halves; score tops 3 times. Place eggplant in a baking pan, cut sides up. Bake for 25 minutes.

While eggplant bakes, spray a medium frying pan with non-sticky spray. Sauté onion for 5 minutes. Add raisins, almonds, cilantro, salt and pepper. Cook over medium-low heat for 5 minutes, stirring frequently.

Remove eggplant from oven. Lower oven heat to 350 degrees. Scoop out eggplant pulp, reserving shells. Chop pulp. Mix with rice and raisin mixture. Stuff pulp mix into eggplant shells. Bake for 15 minutes.

Meanwhile, make tomato curry sauce: in a medium saucepan, mix all sauce ingredients. Cook over medium-low heat until tomatoes are soft and saucy, stirring occasionally.

To serve, spoon sauce over stuffed eggplant shells.

Serves 1

Calories:
wild rice - 289
raisins - 225
almonds - 150
honey - 64
728 total

Wilted Spinach Nectarine Salad

2 bunches fresh spinach, stems removed

1 nectarine, chopped

1/2 lb. (1 1/2 c.) jicama, skinned and chopped

non-stick vegetable spray

2 T. olive oil

1 onion, finely chopped

1 t. honey

1 t. Dijon mustard

2 T. cider vinegar

1/4 t. black pepper

1/4 c. vegetarian baco bits

1 egg, hard-boiled and chopped

Wash and drain spinach in colander. Pat leaves dry with paper towels. Mix spinach with nectarine and jicama.

Spray a large frying pan with non-stick spray. Begin to heat pan, then add oil. Over medium-low heat sauté onion until lightly browned and tender. Stir in honey, mustard, vinegar, and pepper. Add spinach mixture to pan. Cover frying pan and cook over low heat for 1 minute. Stir well to mix flavors then add baco bits, cover pan again, and cook for 1 more minute. (Spinach should be warm and soft-crunchy.)

Toss salad into a wooden serving bowl. Sprinkle salad top with egg.

Serves 1

Calories:
nectarine - 80

oil - 240
honey - 22
baco bits - 96
egg - 80
518 total

Zesty Potatoes With Broiled Tomatoes

2 baking potatoes

1/4 lb. mushrooms, sliced

1 green onion, chopped

1/4 pkg. (3.5 oz.) tofu, mashed

1/4 c. ketchup (a brand made with honey, preferably)

1/4 t. Dijon mustard

1 1/2 t. lemon Juice

1 t. tamari

1/2 t. salt (optional)

1/4 t. black pepper

1/4 c. plus 1 T. vegetarian baco bits

4 tomatoes, halved

garlic powder

salt (optional)

Basil

Preheat oven to 450 degrees.

Bake potatoes for 1 hour or until tender Inside.

Meanwhile, steam mushrooms and green onion for 8-10 minutes or until soft. Blend tofu, ketchup, mustard, lemon juice, and tamari until smooth. Mix one-half of tofu sauce with steamed mushrooms and green onions, along with 1/2 t. salt, black pepper, and 1/4 c. baco bits; reserve other half of tofu sauce. Set mushroom mix and reserved sauce aside.

Remove potatoes from oven. Cut off tops, scoop out insides of potatoes. Mash potato pulp; mix with mushroom mix until well-blended. Place potato shells in a baking pan.

Re-stuff with mushroom mixture; top with reserved sauce. Replace potato tops. Bake for 10 minutes.

Change oven setting to broil. Place tomato halves on a broiler pan. Sprinkle lightly with garlic powder, salt, basil, and remaining 1 T. baco bits. Broil 15 minutes until soft with crispy tops. (Note: to keep potatoes warm while tomatoes broil, place potato baking pan underneath the tomatoes in the oven- i.e. on the lower rack.)

Serve potatoes and tomatoes side by side.

Serves 1

Calories:
potato - 290
tofu - 85
ketchup - 64
baco bits - 120
559 total

Zucchini Pie Filled
With Mushroom and Pearl Onion Creole

3 zucchini, grated

1 c. puffed rice, wheat, or millet (unsweetened), crushed

1 egg, beaten

1/4 t. salt (optional)

non-stick vegetable spray

1/2 lb. mushrooms, sliced

10 oz. pearl onions, skins removed

4 tomatoes, chopped

1/2 c. distilled water

1 green bell pepper, thinly sliced

3/4 t. salt (optional)

1/4 t. paprika

3/4 t. curry powder

1 T. honey

1 1/2 T. whole wheat flour

Preheat oven to 400 degrees.

Place grated zucchini between paper towels and press out moisture. Mix zucchini with cereal, egg, and 1/4 t. salt. Spray a pie plate with non-stick spray. Press zucchini mixture into pie plate and up edges. Bake for 45 minutes or until light brown with crispy edges.

Meanwhile, put rest of ingredients, except flour, in a medium saucepan. Bring to a boil then lower heat and simmer, uncovered, for 10 minutes, stirring occasionally. Slowly mix in flour. Simmer, uncovered, for 10 more minutes.

To serve, pour pearl onion Creole Into zucchini pie crust.

Serves 1

Calories:
cereal - 50 (may vary slightly among cereals)
egg - 80
honey - 64
flour - 38
232 total

Variation:

~Instead of filling zucchini pie with Creole, use one-half of ratatouille recipe.

Equivalents

The following equivalents, cooking times, and amounts are approximated to help you when you prepare meals. Foods, stoves, cooking implements and other variables might cause slight variations in my figures.

Dry Weights and Measures

dash or pinch	=	less than 1/8 teaspoons
3 teaspoons	=	1 tablespoon
4 tablespoons	=	1/4 cup
1/3 cup	=	5 1/3 tablespoons
1/2 cup	=	8 tablespoon
3/4 cup	=	12 tablespoons
1 cup	=	16 tablespoons
1 pound	=	16 ounces

LIquid Weights and Measures

3 teaspoons	=	1 tablespoon
2 tablespoons	=	1 fluid ounce
4 tablespoons	=	1/4 cup
1/3 cup	=	5 1/3 tablespoons
1/2 cup	=	8 tablespoons
1/2 cup	=	4 fluid ounces
3/4 cup	=	12 tablespoons
1 cup	=	16 tablespoons
1 cup	=	8 fluid ounces
1 cup	=	1/2 pint
4 cups	=	1 quart
1 quart	=	32 fluid ounces
4 quarts	=	1 gallon

Equivalent Amounts of Same Foods
in Different Form

Food	Amount	Equivalent Amount
Almonds:		
unshelled	1 pound	= 1 1/4 c. nutmeats
shelled	1 pound	= 4 1/4 c. nutmeats
Apples:	1 pound (3 med.)	= 3 c. raw, sliced
	1 pound	= 2/3 c. chopped. steamed
	1 pound	= 1 1/4 c. pureed
Apricots	1 pound	= 3 1/4 c. dried
Bananas	1 pound (3 lg.)	= 1 3/4 c. mashed
Bell peppers, red or green	1 large	= 1 c. chopped
Brazil Nuts:		
unshelled	1 pound	= 1 1/2 c. nutmeats
shelled	1 pound	= 3 c. nutmeats
Bread:		
dry	1 slice	= 1/3 c. fine crumbs
fresh	1 slice	= 1/2 c. soft crumbs

Food	Amount		Equivalent Amount
Brown rice, raw	1 cup	=	3 c. cooked
Buckwheat groats.			
raw	1 cup	=	3 c. cooked
Bulgar, raw	1 cup	=	3 c. cooked
Cabbage, raw	1 pound	=	4 1/4 c. shredded
Carrots, raw:	1 pound	=	3 c. shredded
	1 pound	=	4 c. diced
Celery, raw	1 pound	=	4 c. diced
Coconut	3 1/2 ounces	=	1 c. grated
Corn, fresh	6 ears	=	1 1/2 c. cut
Cornmeal, dry	1 pound	=	3 c. dry
	1 cup	=	3 c. cooked
Eggs, hard-boiled	6 medium	=	1 1/2 c. chopped
Garlic	1 clove	=	1/4 tsp. powder
Herbs			
fresh,chopped	1 tbsp.	=	1 tsp. dried
Hiziki seaweed, dried	1/4 cup	=	1 c. re-hydrated

Food	Amount		Equivalent Amount
Kidney beans, dry:			
	1 pound	=	2 1/2 c. dry
	1 cup	=	2 c. cooked
Lemon:	1 medium	=	3 tbsp. Juice
	1 medium	=	1 1/2 tsp. rind. grated
Lentils, dry:	1 pound	=	2 1/4 c. dry
	1 pound	=	5 c. cooked
Lima beans, dry:	1 pound	=	2 1/2 c. dry
	1 cup	=	2 1/2 c. cooked
Macaroni, un-cooked	1 pound	=	4 c. raw
	1 cup	=	2 c. cooked
Mushrooms, raw	1/2 pound	=	3 c. sliced
Navy beans, dry:	1 pound	=	2 1/2 c. dry
	1 cup	=	2 1/2 c. cooked
Noodles, un-cooked:	1 pound	=	6 c. raw
	1 cup	=	2 c. cooked
Oats, rolled:	1 pound	=	6 1/4 c. raw
	1 cup	=	1 3/4 c. cooked

Food	Amount		Equivalent Amount
Onion, raw	1 medium	=	1/2 c. minced
Orange:	1 medium	=	1/2 c. juice
	1 medium	=	1 1/2 tbsp. rind, grated
Parsley, fresh, chopped	1/4 cup	=	1 tbsp. dried
Peas, in pods	1 pound	=	1 c. shelled
Peanuts:			
unshelled	1 pound	=	2 c. nutmeats
shelled	1 pound	=	4 1/2 c. nutmeats
Potatoes, raw	3 medium	=	1 3/4 c. mashed
Raisins	1 pound	=	2 3/4 c.
Sesame seeds	2 tbsp.	=	1 tbsp. tahini (sesame paste)
Spinach, raw	1 pound	=	1 1/2 c. cooked
Strawberries	1 pint	=	1 1/2 c. sliced
Sunflower seeds, shelled	2 tbsp.	=	1 tbsp. sunflower butter
Walnuts:			
unshelled	1 pound	=	1 3/4 c. nutmeats
shelled	1 pound	=	4 1/2 c. nutmeats

Food	Amount		Equivalent Amount
Wheat germ	12 ounces	=	3 c.
White beans, raw	1 cup	=	2 1/2 c. cooked
Whole wheat flour	1 pound	=	3 3/4 c.
Wild rice, raw	1 cup	=	3 c. cooked

Equivalent Substitutions - Foods

Food	Amount	Substitute Food
Arrowroot	1 1/2 tsp. =	1 tbsp. flour
	1 tbsp. =	1 tbsp. cornstarch
Butter	1 cup =	7/8 c. vegetable oil
Cayenne Pepper	1/8 tsp. =	3-4 drops liquid hot pepper
Chocolate	1 ounce =	3 tbsp. carob pwd. plus 2 tbsp. water
Cornstarch	1 tbsp. =	2 tbsp. flour
	1 tbsp. =	1 tbsp. arrowroot
Cracker crumbs	3/4 cup =	1 c. whole grain bread crumbs
Egg	1 whole =	1 tbsp. liquid lecithin
Flour	2 tbsp. =	1 tbsp. cornstarch
	2 tbsp. =	1 tbsp. arrowroot
Lemon Juice	1 tsp. =	1/2-1 tsp. vinegar
Mustard, prepared	1 tbsp. =	1 tsp. dry mustard
Soy sauce	1 tbsp. =	1 tbsp. tamari
Tomatoes, chopped	1 cup =	1/2 c. water plus 1/2 c. tomato sauce

Equivalent Substitutions - Herbs and Spices

Herb or Spice	Possible Substitutes
Capers	Pickles, pickled green pepper.
Caraway	Anise seed
Cardamom	Coriander, ginger
Cayenne pepper	Chill powder
Celery seed	Celery leaves, chopped
Chervil	Tarragon
Chives	Scallions
Cilantro	Italian parsley
Cinnamon	Allspice, nutmeg
Cloves	Cinnamon, ginger
Coriander	Cardamom, ginger
Cumin	Turmeric
Dill	Caraway
Fennel	Anise
Fenugreek	Anise, caraway, fennel
Ginger	Cardamom, coriander
Mace	Nutmeg
Marjoram	Basil, oregano, thyme

Herb or Spice	Possible Substitutes
Mint	Bay leaf
Mustard powder	Prepared mustard
Nutmeg	Cinnamon, mace
Oregano	Basil, marjoram, thyme
Parsley	Basil
Pepper	Cayenne Pepper, red pepper
Rosemary	Mint, sage
Saffron	Turmeric
Sage	Rosemary, savory
Savory	Sage
Tarragon	Chervil
Thyme	Basil, marjoram, oregano
Turmeric	Cumin

Cooking Grains

Dry Grain (1 Cup Dry)	Cooking Time (Approx.)	Cooking Water	Cooked Volume	Possible Substitute
Amaranth	25 minutes	3 cups	2 1/2 cups	millet, sorghum
Barley	55 minutes	3 cups	3 cups	brown rice, wheat
Buckwheat groats	15 minutes	5 cups	4 cups	oats, bulgur
Cornmeal	25 minutes	4 cups	3 cups	amaranth, millet
Millet	45 minutes	3 cups	3 1/2 cups	amaranth, cornmeal, sorghum
Oats	35 minutes	3 cups	1 3/4 cups	buckwheat
Rice, brown	40 minutes	2 cups	3 cups	barley, wild rice
Rice, wild	50 minutes	3 cups	3 cups	barley. brown rice
Rye berries	60 minutes	4 cups	2 2/3 cups	triticale, wheat berry
Sorghum	45 minutes	3 cups	3 1/2 cups	amaranth, millet
Triticale	60 minutes	4 cups	2 1/2 cups	rye, wheat
Wheat berries	2 hours	3 cups	2 2/3 cups	rye, triticale
Wheat, cracked	25 minutes	2 cups	2 1/3 cups	brown rice, buckwheat, rye, triticale
Wheat, bulgur	20 minutes	2 cups	2 1/2 cups	brown rice, buckwheat, rye, triticale

Cooking Legumes

Dried Beans (1 cup dry)	Cooking Time (approx)	Cooking Water	Cooked Volume	Possible Substitute
Adzuki bean	45 minutes	4 cups	2 1/2 cups	mung, soybeans
Black-eyed pea	1 hour	4 cups	2 1/2 cups	white bean
Chick pea (garbanzo)	2 hours	4 cups	3 1/4 cups	fava bean
Fava bean	50 minutes	4 cups	2 1/2 cups	lima bean
Kidney bean	1 1/2 hours	3 cups	2 1/2 cups	pinto bean
Lentil	30 minutes	4 cups	2 3/4 cups	split pea
Lima bean	50 minutes	4 cups	2 1/2 cups	fava bean
Mung bean	1 1/2 hours	4 cups	2 1/2 cups	adzuki bean, soybean
Pea, split	35 minutes	3 cups	2 1/4 cups	lentil
Pinto bean	1 1/2 hours	3 cups	2 cups	black bean, kidney bean
Soybean	3 hours	5 cups	2 3/4 cups	adzuki bean, mung bean
White beans	50 minutes	4 cups	2 3/4 cups	kidney bean, lima bean

About the Author

Jennifer Stang was born in New York and grew up in a beautiful beach town in Los Angeles, California. With an artistic soul, Jennifer always enjoyed food, its textures, shapes, colors, and flavors. In her teens, Jen's overindulgence in food -- which diverted her from her tenderness -- led her to seek weight loss plans, all of which were meat-based. Then, at age 19, Jennifer had an epiphany: after yelling at a cat for killing a bird she realized that she was a hypocrite, eating dead animals for almost every dinner. With a profound love, compassion, and respect for animals, Jennifer decided she could never find health through the death of another creature. She became vegetarian.

After trying endless vegetarian diets -- many of which led her to weight gain -- Jennifer developed a marvelous system for losing weight while feeling happy, healthy, and full. She transformed her body with her Santa Barbara Diet, losing 50 pounds. She kept her recipes dairyless, as well, to further ensure health. While many people believed that eliminating meat from a diet would cause poor health and fragility, Jen enjoyed high energy from lighter, more digestible foods, running 9-12 miles a day and competing in sports.

Now, 27 years later, Jennifer is still vegetarian, youthful, and extremely energetic and fit from her healthy diet and lifestyle. Now an author, landscape artist and sculptor, she lives on 1¼ acres with her family and many animal friends. Her three children are all vegetarian from birth and also enjoy great health and cherish life in all forms.

Jennifer's latest book, "Ally & Oops," is an illustrated storybook that teaches children the joys of caring for their animal friends. It's a wonderful gift when a child asks, "Can I have a puppy?"

Further Reading

Find these and other titles from William Baughman Publishing

The Secret Tao
By D.W. Kreger

Thank You,
Tony Robbins
by Manny Ibay

The Tao of Yoda
By D.W. Kreger

Ally & Oops
by Jennifer Stang